American Woodworker

Getting *the* Most *from your* Wood-Buying Bucks

American Woodworker

Getting *the* Most *from your* Wood-Buying Bucks

Find, Cut, and Dry Your Own Lumber

FOX CHAPEL
PUBLISHING

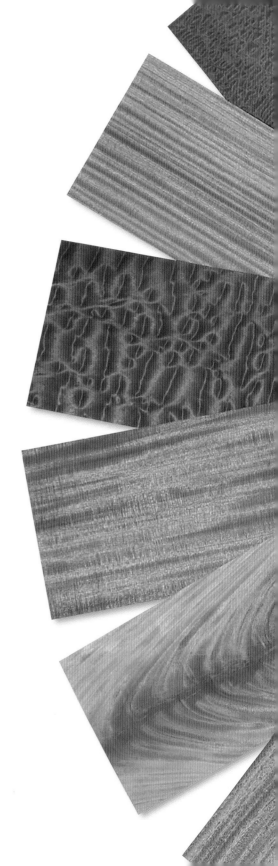

Published by Fox Chapel Publishing Company, Inc., 1970 Broad St., East Petersburg, PA 17520, 717-560-4703, www.FoxChapelPublishing.com

American Woodworker, ISSN 1074-9152, USPS 738-710, is published bimonthly by Woodworking Media, LLC, 90 Sherman St., Cambridge, MA 02140, www.AmericanWoodworker.com.

Library of Congress Control Number: 2009053474
ISBN-13: 978-1-56523-460-4
ISBN-10: 1-56523-460-X

Library of Congress Cataloging-in-Publication Data

Getting the most from your wood-buying bucks

   p. cm.

Includes index.

ISBN 978-1-56523-460-4

1. Woodwork. 2. Wood--indentification. 3. Wood products--Purchasing. Fox Chapel Publishing.

TT180.G48 2010

684'.080681--dc22

2009053474

To learn more about the other great books from Fox Chapel Publishing, or to find a retailer near you, call toll-free 800-457-9112 or visit us at *www. FoxChapelPublishing.com.*

Printed in China
First printing: April 2010

Contents

What You Can Learn

Finding Great Wood

You can buy domestic and imported hardwoods, surface-planed and ready to saw and use, at the home center or woodworking retailer. But you will pay a premium price for the service. When money is tight you can find better wood for lower prices, if you're willing to do some of that work yourself. Here are some choices:

- Look for small local sawmills that buy logs and convert them to lumber. You can buy rough, unseasoned wood for big price discounts. You'll have to sticker and stack the wood until it dries, and you'll have to plane it yourself, but you'll save big bucks.

- Look for local dealers in reclaimed timber. These folks take down old houses, factories and barns, pull the paint off the wood and the nails out of it, and re-sell it. You might not save a lot of money, but you'll gain a lot in quality.

- Look for tree services whose main business is logging and tree removal. These folks can sell you logs that you can arrange to have sawn at a small local sawmill, and some of them offer sawmilling services themselves.

- Learn how to spot the great wood in piles of ordinary, low-grade lumber. You'll put in your own time and labor, but you'll end up with high-quality material at a bargain price.

❮ **Gold in those piles of boards**—*Lumber grading rules are both complex and oriented to industrial needs. That's why this dude could find such beautiful wood in a big stack of No. 2 lumber. He had to do the work of picking through the stack and piling it up neatly, but what a deal!*

by DAVE MUNKITTRICK

Finding Great Wood

AMAZING WOOD AT FANTASTIC PRICES HARVESTED CLOSE TO HOME

When I built my solar kiln (see page 98), I needed to scour up a steady source for green wood to dry. Turns out it wasn't as hard as I thought. I live about an hour outside of a major metropolitan area and a little digging in the Yellow Pages turned up a wealth of green wood sources. I found everything from ordinary basswood to spectacular maple crotches, to enormous walnut trunks. All were at unbelievable prices. I began my search in the Yellow Pages with calls to custom sawyers with portable sawmills. They put me on to a couple of good sources for green wood, which included private tree services and municipal maintenance departments. They have a ton of wood and some of it is quite amazing.

Finding green wood may take a little digging, but you'll find your sources will grow naturally. My first contact quickly blossomed into several other contacts. Before I knew it, I was reluctantly turning down offers for wood because I simply had no place to store it.

Custom Sawyers

I visited a small custom sawmill, Dan's Wood Service, located in western Wisconsin. I was looking for an easy-to-dry wood for the a test run in my solar kiln. Dan offered me some clear basswood for seventy cents per bd. ft. That's about a third of the cost my local lumberyard charges for kiln-dried wood. I took a friend along for help with the stacking.

When we got to Dan's place I was surprised to learn that my wood was a standing tree in his woodlot! Dan harvested it in no time (photo 1, page 14). The tree trunks were then cut to length (photo 2, page 15) and transported to the nearby sawmill on the property (photo 3, page 15). Sizeable tree trunks are really heavy and present the most difficult material-handling dilemma for folks like you and me. Fortunately, most custom sawyers like Dan are set up to bring their mill to your tree so there's no need for skid loaders, huge trucks and big cranes.

The bandsaw mill made quick work of our tree (photo 4, page 15). An in-line

No big logging truck—Portable bandsaw mills like this Wood Mizer have changed the sawmilling equation. The big advantage is, you tow the portable bandsaw to the logs, then you haul the sawn boards away. The big diesel logging truck and the huge stationary circular saw don't enter the picture.

Urban Lumber

Harvest great wood in the heart of the city

by SETH KELLER

I live right in the heart of the city. By accident, I found great wood right under my nose, in the midst of a bustling metropolis. My first adventure as an urban lumberjack began with a phone call from a friend telling me that an old red oak in his backyard was struck by lightning and was bound for the chipper.

"Do you want it?" he asked. "I'll be right over," was my reply. I borrowed a Logosol portable sawmill from a friend and headed over to my buddy's backyard.

Once word got out that I could turn doomed trees into useful lumber, I had more offers for free wood than I could handle.

A friend called me about a red oak tree he had to take down. The main trunk was nine feet tall, weighed over 1500 lbs. and was about to hit the ground when I arrived with a portable sawmill.

Let the fun begin! Getting the log up the ramp and onto the sawmill was a bit of work, but once in place, sawing the log into planks was pretty simple. It's about 10 minutes per slice, though.

This log was over 26 inches wide! Each cut was like opening a present: I never knew what to expect, but I was never disappointed. It was particularly fun to see quartersawn pieces emerge from the log.

Within a week of sawing my first tree, I got a call about a downed birch. This tree had some amazing figure, especially near the base. Every tree I cut is a treasure. I never lose that sense of wonder as a beautiful plank is cut loose from a tree that would otherwise be destined for the chipper.

ripsaw took care of the bark edges (photo 5, right). Soon we had the wood stacked in the trailer and were on our way back to the kiln (photo 6, page 16). Believe it or not–from tree to trailer took less than two hours. I was amazed.

Tree Service Boneyards

We checked out a local tree service's boneyard to see what was available. Tree services and municipalities are no longer allowed to burn their trees or take them to landfills. Commercial mills aren't interested in trees from populated areas where human activity leads to buried nails in tree trunks that ruin a sawyers' day. So where do all those trees go? They go to the boneyard, where most are chopped into mulch. It's kinda like an animal shelter for trees. If no one comes to take them away, well…it's the chipper.

Boneyards toss out an amazing amount of wood every day (photo 7, page 16). A little poking around yielded spectacular finds including maple, oak and walnut (photo 8, page 16). The service was reluctant to let us bring a mill onto their property for liability reasons. However, they were amenable to dropping the logs off at my shop where a mill could be brought in later. Now my biggest problem is finding a place to store all this wood. I'd better start building some furniture!

I was looking for some green wood for my kiln but never dreamed the wood I ordered would be cut on the spot. Dan is a custom sawyer who specializes in small orders. He has a small woodlot where he harvests trees like this basswood. His portable sawmill can travel to you and your tree wherever you are.

Dan cut the felled tree into 8½ ft. lengths for the sawmill. He left a large shoot growing from the stump. A basswood shoot will grow to become a mature tree that can be re-harvested in another 10-20 years.

A skid loader picks up and carries the heavy logs to a portable sawmill set up on the property. For off-site work, Dan brings the sawmill right to the tree.

The basswood logs are cut into boards on a bandsaw mill. I found several sawyers with portable mills like this in the Yellow Pages.

A ripsaw removes the bark edge leaving two straight edges. This makes stacking for drying a lot easier because you don't have the uneven bark edge to deal with. You can use your own bandsaw to remove a bark edge, too.

My buddy and I load the boards onto my trailer. The basswood went from tree to trailer in less than two hours. Green wood can deteriorate rapidly so we wasted little time getting back home in order to stack the wood for drying.

The following week we stopped at a local tree service boneyard where a constant stream of trucks brought in a ton of brush and branches and more than a few prize logs. I wished I could have cut them up on the spot to see what kind of great wood was getting tossed out.

We found some amazing trees destined to get chipped into mulch. A little bargaining can land you some fantastic deals on some fantastic wood. It just takes a little poking around to get the ball rolling. We had Dan saw up some of the logs we found here.

by GEORGE VONDRISKA

Reclaimed Timber

FOR AN INSTANT ANTIQUE, TRY RECYCLED WOOD!

ART DIRECTION: BARBARA PEDERSON • PHOTOGRAPHY: MIKE HABERMANN

Wood doesn't just grow on trees, you know. It also comes from barns, warehouses, factories and railroad trestles that are being torn down. This wood, called reclaimed timber, just might be an alternative material you can use.

Reclaimed timber offers some unique opportunities. Because of its original application, the boards probably have a lot of "character." This means nail, screw and even bolt holes. Instead of trying to work around and eliminate them, you might try using them to give the project a unique look.

The wood itself is different, too. This lumber was almost always cut from old-growth trees. These trees grew very slowly in dense forests. The resulting growth rings are close together, making the wood more dense and stable. In addition, today's softwoods are dried to around 12- to 14-percent moisture content, making it unsuitable for cabinets and furniture. This old stuff is generally drier than that.

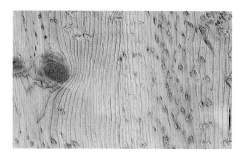
Bird's Eye Pine

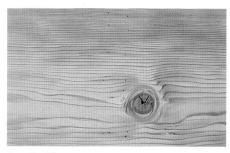
Douglas Fir

Most suppliers are able to attach a history to the reclaimed timber they sell. Not only can you create a unique piece, you'll also be able to identify what building, city and era it came from.

Salvage wood from old buildings is primarily softwood. You'll find

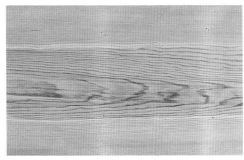

Bird's Eye Pine

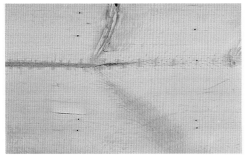

Douglas Fir

southern yellow pine, redwood, Douglas fir, ponderosa pine, incense cedar, oak and even bird's eye pine, to name a few. Species availability varies, because the salvage companies take whatever they can find.

In its first life, the wood may have been used for anything from flooring to shelving to structural beams. Metal detectors are used to find and remove hardware. Timber coming from flooring and shelving, commonly 4/4 to 8/4, is generally abrasive planed (sanded to thickness) and sold by the board foot in random length and width lots. Large beams may be sold as beams, or resawn to a customer's specifications.

It's a good idea to let the supplier do the abrasive planing for you. Lead-based paint was used in the United States until 1978, and having the planing done by the supplier

keeps any potentially toxic waste out of your life. Once you have the wood in your shop, using standard dust control procedures should be adequate.

You might find reclaimed timber more brittle than other wood. You'll also want to keep an eye out for hardware and fasteners, even if you had the supplier do this for you. Other than that, it works like any other material you're accustomed to.

Prices on reclaimed timber can range tremendously, from 50 cents to $12 per board foot. Price fluctuations are caused by the logistics of salvaging the wood, its condition after salvage and supply and demand. Material selection, quantity purchased and shipping charges also affect your final cost.

Reclaimed timber marries the old to the new. It's reasonably priced and gives you the opportunity to creatively work with, not around, the wood's rich history.

Second time around—This lovely room was built using reclaimed timber: big Douglas fir ceiling beams from a demolished factory, with wide, knotty white pine for the floor and wall paneling. You'd have a tough time finding new boards as pretty as these.

Southern Yellow Heart Pine

Four Ways Wood Distorts

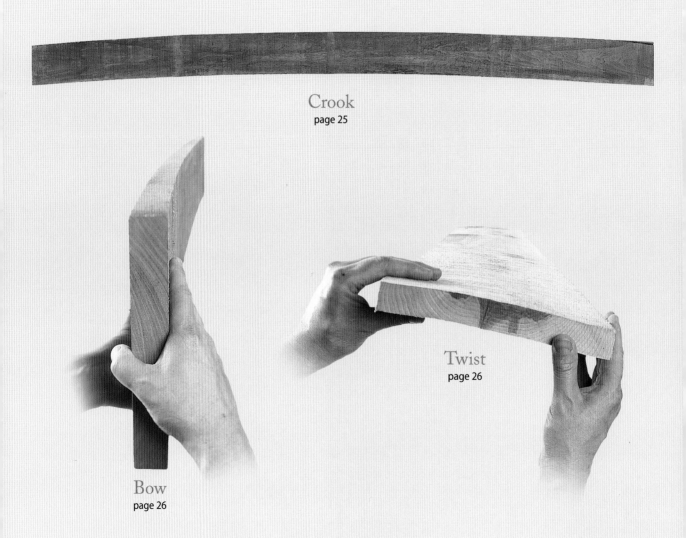

Cup
page 25

Crook
page 25

Bow
page 26

Twist
page 26

By TIM JOHNSON

Buying and Using Rough Lumber

BUY SMART TO GET THE BEST DEALS AND THE BEST WOOD

Start Out Thick

Rough lumber thicknesses are measured in ¼-in. increments. The thinnest rough-cut boards, labeled 4/4, and called four quarter, are 1-in. thick.

It's tough to get surfaced stock thicker than $^{13}/_{16}$-in. from 1-in. rough stock. Plan to lose $^3/_{16}$-in. (¼-in. on thicker stock) when you plane a roughsawn board smooth.

Hardwood lumberyards commonly stock species in 4/4 and 8/4 thicknesses, with additional sizes available based on supply and demand.

Buy More than Enough

It's a big mistake to buy the exact amount of wood your project requires. If you do, you're gonna come up short, because rough lumber isn't perfect, not even top-grade boards.

A common rule of thumb is to buy 15 to 20 percent more than you need. Some species, like red oak, consistently contain few defects, so you don't have to over-buy

1" 4/4
1¼" 5/4
1½" 6/4
2" 8/4
2½" 10/4
3" 12/4
4" 16/4

STAFF

Be Prepared

Take a tape measure and calculator with you when you go to the lumberyard so you can measure the boards you choose and figure out how much they'll cost. Because roughsawn boards come in random widths and lengths (no two are alike) they're measured by volume, which can be calculated by using a simple formula. The standard unit, a board foot (bd. ft.), measures 12-in. x 12-in. x 1-in.-thick, or 144 cubic inches.

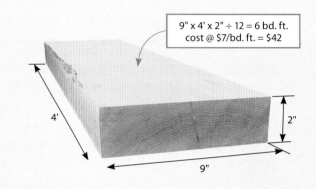

1 bd. ft.

1"
12"
12"

Width x Length x Thickness ÷ 12 = Board Feet
(in inches)   (in feet)   (in inches)

Because bd. ft. is a measure of volume, any combination of thickness (minimum 1 in.), width and length that equals 144 cubic inches also equals one bd. ft.

Rough lumber is sold based on its cost per bd. ft. Some species are more pricey than others, and thicker boards cost more per bd. ft. than thin ones. To determine cost, simply multiply the total number of bd. ft. in the boards you've selected by the bd. ft. price.

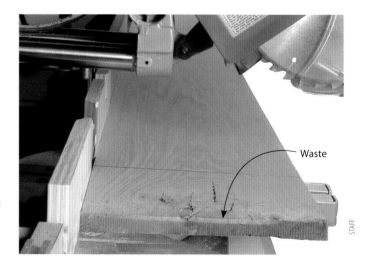

9" x 4' x 2" ÷ 12 = 6 bd. ft.
cost @ $7/bd. ft. = $42

4'
2"
9"

as much. Other species, like black walnut, require more insurance than the average.

I usually don't bother with percentages, I just buy extra pieces. For example, if I'm going to build a table, I'll choose enough stock to make an extra leg. If the top requires seven boards, I'll buy eight.

Buy Long

Don't expect to get an 8-ft. length out of an 8-ft. rough board. Even though roughsawn boards are regularly cut a couple of inches long, they usually contain checks, knots or wild grain that must be cut off. If you need finished 8-ft. lengths, you'll probably have to buy 9- or even 10-ft.-long boards.

Waste

STAFF

$100 of S/B
basswood
30 bd. ft.

$100 of 1C
basswood
46 bd. ft.

Check Out No. 1 Common

No. 1 Common (1C) lumber is always worth considering. It sits only one notch below Selects and Better (S/B), the best grade most lumberyards carry, but costs up to 40 percent less.

In general, 1C grade has more defects, and boards usually contain more waste. This reduces its cost advantage somewhat. On the other hand, some 1C boards are perfect, but too narrow or short to make S/B grade. In fact, there's a large gray area between the low end of S/B lumber and the top end of 1C lumber. It's not hard to find 1C boards that look just as good, if not better, than S/B boards. Buying 1C lumber is a great way to stretch your woodworking dollars.

TUBULAR STORAGE

Here's my solution for storing skinny things like wood trim and edge banding. I bought a 12-in.-dia. by 8-ft.-long cardboard concrete form at a home center for about $14. I slid plywood dividers into the tube and added a few screws to hold the dividers in place. I hung it from the ceiling in my basement with plumber's strap. Get plumber's strap at a home center for about $2 for a 10-ft. roll. It took one roll to hang my storage tube.

George R. HOFFMAN

Top-Grade Boards Aren't Always Pretty

Spectacular boards cost no more than ordinary ones, because lumber grades depend on yield, not aesthetics. The presence of off-color sapwood and funny-looking figure isn't a factor. The four boards below all came from the same top-grade stack. In the eyes of the grader, the trio of slender boards is identical to the single wide one, because they contain the same amount of usable material. Three boards or one, they'll cost the same. How would you spend your money?

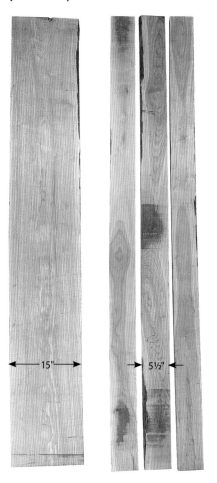

← 15" →   → 5½" ←

Tame Warped Lumber

Common sense tells you to choose flat boards and avoid the pretzels. Unfortunately, flat roughsawn boards are sometimes hard to find. Lots of boards end up warped as a result of the drying process. In lumber lingo, warp is defined as any deflection from a flat, planar surface. Warped boards can be cupped, bowed, crooked or twisted. A single board can contain a combination of warps.

Luckily, most warped boards can be flattened, if the deflection isn't too severe. Knowing how to identify and deal with boards that aren't perfectly flat will give you many more choices as you look through the stack.

For more information on No. 1 Common lumber, see page 23.

Cup

A board that bends across the width of its face is cupped. Cupping, which occurs mainly in plainsawn lumber, affects a board's finished thickness.

Boards that are slightly cupped are easy to flatten. Joint them with the concave side down. This keeps both outside edges in contact with the jointer's bed, for stability. To flatten a severely cupped board without sacrificing its thickness, rip it in half and joint both pieces separately. Don't rip a cupped board on your tablesaw, however. It's too likely to cause a kickback. Use a bandsaw, circular saw, or jigsaw. Glue the pieces back together, after jointing their mating edges. Then make a final smoothing pass on the glued-up face.

Cut far from center

Cut close to center

Cupping is more likely on plainsawn boards cut close to the center of the tree. Boards showing wide, shallow arcs are best. Cupping almost always occurs on the bark side of the board, away from the center.

Crook

A board that bends along its length is crooked. Straightening a crooked board reduces its width. Boards with a minor crook are common. They can be straightened by jointing and/or ripping. (Don't rip a crooked board on the tablesaw without a sled to hold it; kickback is too likely.) Jointing or ripping won't work on a board with a major crook— you'd end up with nothing. Instead, cut the board into short pieces.

Check for cup by looking at the end of the board.

A crooked board makes a smiley (or frowny) face.

Minor crook can be straightened.

Major crook must be crosscut, then straightened.

Bow is easy to see when you sight down the edge of the board.

Twist

A board with one high corner has twist. It's best to let twisted boards be someone else's nightmare. They're difficult to flatten, and even if you're successful, the twist has a tendency to return. If you must use a twisted board, cut it as short as possible, to minimize the deflection.

Sight down the face of a board. If the opposite ends aren't parallel, it's twisted. Put it back.

Bow

A board that bends across the length of its face is bowed. You'll lose length when you flatten bowed boards, because you have to remove more from the ends than the middle. Joint with the bowed side down, and don't press the board flat against the jointer bed. The only way to deal with a board with a pronounced bow is to cut it into shorter lengths. The short pieces will still bow, but not as much, so they'll be easier to flatten. If the bow is confined to one end of the board, cut it off or make repeated jointing passes on that end only.

Look for Hit-and-Miss

The landscape at the lumberyard is changing because stock surfaced hit-and-miss (H/M) is becoming common, and may eventually replace rough lumber altogether.

H/M planing skins the board's rough surfaces. This makes choosing good-looking boards easier because you can see what they look like, without having to guess. Even though I've been buying rough lumber for

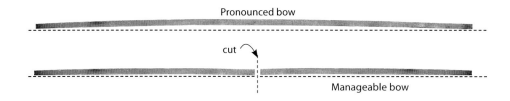

Pronounced bow

cut

Manageable bow

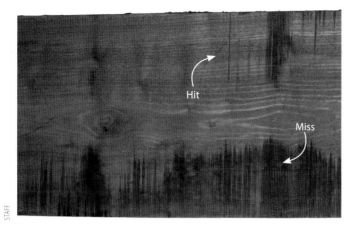

STAFF

Take Advantage of Milling Services

Rough lumber is rarely flat or straight. Milling your own is backbreaking work, takes forever and produces gobs of sawdust.

Why not let the lumberyard do it for you? Most yards will rip one edge of a rough board straight (called SL/E, straight-line edge), plane both faces (S2S, surfaced two sides), or mill both faces and edges (S4S, surfaced four sides). In addition to a setup fee of $15 to $45, the cost ranges from about 15 to 30 cents per bd. ft., depending on which type of milling you choose. It's not worth the expense to have only a few boards milled—for small amounts, it's usually cheaper to head straight to the yard's inventory of surfaced lumber. The set-up fee usually gets waived for large milling jobs, over 150 bd. ft., for example. Check with your yard for specific costs and minimum amounts.

years, I still get fooled. It's just plain hard to see the figure pattern and color in a roughsawn board. H/M planing keeps you from buying ugly boards. H/M boards are also easier on your tools, because the rough top layer, which often contains dirt and other junk, has been removed.

Here's the bad news. First, you've got less thickness to work with. H/M-surfaced boards are $\frac{1}{16}$-in. thinner than the rough thickness (4/4 H/M stock is $\frac{15}{16}$-in. thick). Second, H/M boards still need to be finish-planed. Their surfaces are coarse and usually contain portions that are still rough (hence the name). And third, H/M planing doesn't flatten warped boards.

A straight-line edge cut (sl/e) made at the lumberyard makes ripping and crosscutting at home safer because it gives you a straight side to work from. It also saves you the frustration of trying to joint a long board on a small jointer.

Beware of Ovals

An oval figure pattern on the board's surface signals a change in grain direction that may cause significant tear-out. You'll be planing with the grain on one side of the oval, but going against it on the other, so there's gonna be trouble.

Instead of sanding like mad to get rid of tear-out, use a scraper or hand plane. Check the edge of the board to see how and where the grain changes, then smooth the oval by working from opposite directions, following the grain.

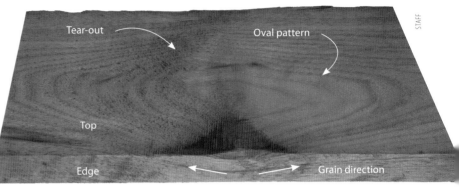

Tear-out

Oval pattern

Top

Edge

Grain direction

STAFF

Edges Reveal the Curl

Spectacular figure may be hidden by a board's roughsawn surface. If you suspect a board contains curly figure, look at its edges for closely spaced light- and dark-colored stripes. Pronounced stripes indicate heavy figure. You can check an entire stack of boards for figured ones just by looking at the stack from the side.

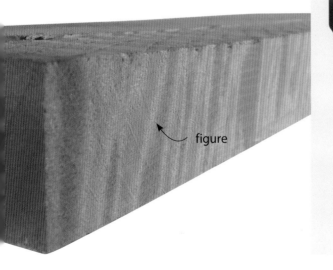

figure

Riftsawn Blank for Legs

For table legs, choose a riftsawn blank; one on which the end grain runs diagonally. Because the blank is riftsawn, all four faces of each leg will exhibit the same straight-grained figure pattern. Look for a blank that's slightly more than twice as wide and slightly more than twice as long as one leg, so you can get all four legs from the same piece.

Riftsawn faces show straight, vertical figure.

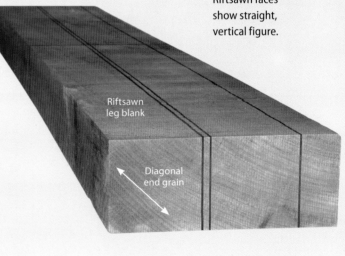

Riftsawn leg blank

Diagonal end grain

STAFF

SAFELY ROUGH-CUT TWISTED LUMBER

by DAVE MUNKITTRICK *and* RICHARD TENDICK

Q: I buy my lumber rough, and sometimes I get a very twisted or crooked board. What's a safe way to crosscut and put a straight edge on these awkward boards?

A: I use a two-step process for safely prepping severely twisted or crooked stock. First I crosscut the board to the desired length with my jigsaw. Then I cut the straight edge on the bandsaw. Of course, the safest way to crosscut rough stock is with a handsaw. Japanese-style utility pull saws designed for fast cutting are ideal for crosscutting rough stock by hand. My tool of choice, though, is a jigsaw with a 4-in., 6-teeth-per-inch (TPI), rough-cutting blade. It's safe to use, gets through the stock quickly and doesn't wear out my arm.

Ripping a straight edge on twisted stock with a large crook is best done on your bandsaw; it's safe and simple. After crosscutting, I use a carpenter's chalk line to mark the straight edge. I take care to position the line to preserve the best parts of the board with the least waste. The chalk line is easy to follow on a bandsaw. After the straight edge is cut, I'm ready to head to the jointer to face-joint the board and clean up the bandsawn edge.

For boards that are not twisted, you have several other options for crosscutting that will get the job done faster. A circular saw makes quick work of trimming rough stock. Sliding miter saws also have the capacity to cut wide boards, as do radial-arm saws.

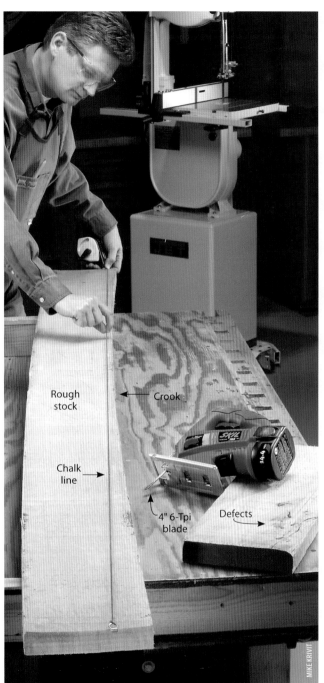

Rough stock

Crook

Chalk line

4" 6-Tpi blade

Defects

MIKE KRIVIT

EDITOR: DAVE MUNKITTRICK • ART DIRECTION: RICK DUPRE • PHOTOGRAPHY: PATRICK HUNTER, UNLESS NOTED

Do-It-Yourself Butcherblock

Butcherblock tops are best made from quartersawn wood, so they don't expand and contract as much. Instead of buying or searching out quartersawn wood, simply buy plainsawn. After milling your boards smooth on top and bottom, rip them in half and rotate both pieces 90 degrees.

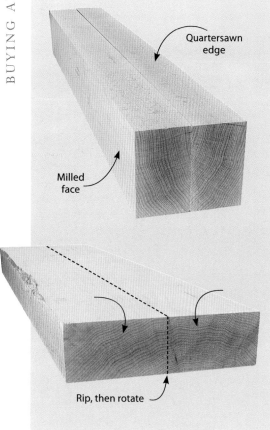

Quartersawn edge

Milled face

Rip, then rotate

Resawing Saves Money and Material

Even though thicker wood costs more, you can save money by using it effectively. Say you need two ½-in.-thick panels. Instead of milling two pieces of 4/4 stock, and wasting almost half of each board, resaw a pair of panels from a single piece of 6/4. Besides, resawing produces bookmatched pieces that can make a great-looking pair of doors.

Be Fussy About Color

One off-color board can ruin the appearance of an entire project. Trust me, that dark (or light) board will bug you every time you see it! You can usually tell when boards don't match, even in the rough. Stand them alongside one another in good natural light, so you can compare.

by TIM JOHNSON AND ED KRAUSE

The Virtues of No. 1 Common

SAVE MONEY BY USING BOARDS THAT AREN'T PERFECT

Defects don't make a board defective; just cheaper. If your project calls for small parts, like stiles and rails, lumber that's graded No. 1 Common is an economical choice. You can harvest perfectly good pieces by cutting around the knots.

Want to make your head spin? Just try to figure out how hardwood lumber is graded. Lumber is such an incredibly diverse material that there are enough grades, rules for grading and exceptions to the rules to make you dizzy. Professional lumber graders use standards, administered by the National Hardwood Lumber Association, to classify every board. While you don't need to be a pro, knowing the difference between No. 1 Common and the higher "select" grades can keep you from wasting your money.

Everybody likes to buy "the best." But when choosing lumber, it's a mistake to pay top dollar for big, clear boards if you're going to cut them up into small pieces. The best boards to buy aren't always the most expensive ones.

No. 1 Common Is Great For Furniture

Take a look at No. 1 Common lumber. It costs a lot less than the higher grades because the boards are smaller and they've got some knots and other defects.

They also contain a lot of perfectly clear material. You just have to be willing to buy a little extra stock and spend some time working with it. It can be a challenge to figure out how to harvest the pieces you need, but it's also enjoyable and rewarding when you do.

No. 1 Common lumber is well suited to furniture making. It's an economical source for narrow stock, perfect for moldings, or stiles and rails for face frames and frame-and-panel structures like doors or cabinet sides. You'll also find boards in the common pile that are wide, with enough clear lengths between defects to make good-looking panels, cabinet sides or small tabletops.

You Can Find Treasure Boards In No. 1 Common

No. 1 Common lumber often contains striking grain and figure patterns that are usually absent in the select grades. That's because these "abnormalities" often occur around knots and near other natural defects. With selective or innovative cutting, you can remove and showcase them. Or perhaps you prefer a look that includes knots, splits and natural edges. Common grade boards can be downright beautiful, making more expensive higher grade boards look plain by comparison!

Finding Hidden Beauty

Finding hidden beauty in an unsightly board is rewarding and well worth the head-scratching it takes. In spite of serious end checks, an awkward grain pattern and a waney edge, the $8 piece of No. 1 Common walnut shown below contains all the parts for an eye-catching cabinet door. There's straight grain for stiles and rails and a piece that, when resawn, made a great bookmatched panel. No. 1 Common boards often contain unusual grain and interesting color and figure. Because these usually occur around defects, you aren't as likely to find them in the higher (clearer) grades.

BEHIND THE STAIRS STORAGE

In my basement shop every square inch counts! Out of necessity I found a wealth of unused space tucked right under my nose, or should I say feet. That awkward space under the basement steps can easily be turned into a set of deep shelves perfect for storing everything from tools to shop vacuums, and of course, lumber. Help your small shop seem a lot bigger by using this highly underutilized space.

Travis LARSON

The Real Difference: A Pretty Face

When you look at a chart of the various lumber grades (page 37), No. 1 Common appears to be a full step lower than Selects and Better. But look closely—the difference is really only a half step.

First, Selects and Better (the highest grade you're likely to see at most lumberyards) isn't the highest grade. It's a combination of the top three grades (think Selects and Better). To make Selects and Better, boards only need to meet the minimum requirements of Selects.

Second, boards are always graded on both faces. Here's the rub: To grade Selects, only one face of a board has to make the top grade (Firsts and Seconds; another combination). The other face only has to make No. 1 Common. That means the difference between No. 1 Common and Selects and Better is one (good) face!

While having a good face is important, the closeness in quality between these grades, compared with the difference in price, makes No. 1 Common worth considering. Remember, just as some of those expensive Selects and Better boards are going to have one No. 1 Common side, some of the cheaper No. 1 Common boards may have one face that's a gem.

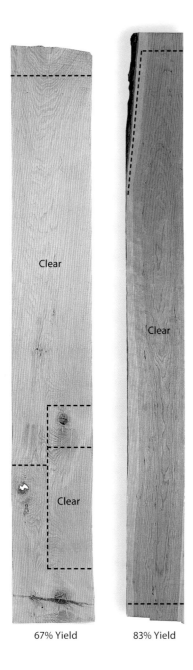

Clear

Clear

Clear

Clear

67% Yield   83% Yield

Expect less clear lumber, but don't be surprised when you get more. No. 1 Common grade allows defects to occupy up to one third of the board. But like any grade, it contains boards that barely qualify (above, left) and boards that just missed being graded higher (above, right).

When Selects And Better Is Better

It makes sense to buy big, defect-free boards for big, smooth surfaces, such as table- or desktops, plank-style cabinet sides or perhaps a head- or footboard. A group of Selects and Better boards may have more consistent color and grain patterns. Defect-free boards are less distracting to look at and generally easier to work with. Working with No. 1 Common takes time and patience.

Some no. 1 Common is very clear, but simply short or narrow. If a board is under 6-ft. long, or less than 4-in. wide, it won't qualify for a higher grade.

ART DIRECTION: PATRICK HUNTER AND SHELLEY MOEN • PHOTOGRAPHY: MIKE HABERMANN

The Nature Of No. 1 Common Lumber

No. 1 Common boards usually come from the interior of large logs or from small logs. The center of a log, or pith, is unusable. Boards cut near the pith contain more defects. Boards from small logs are either narrow or cut close to the pith.

Expect to find these defects, alone or in combination, when you look at No. 1 common:

- **Knots.** The boards are likely to have several knots, clustered, loose or even open.
- **Bark.** There'll be edges containing bark (wane), including up to one third of a board's width and up to half of its length. Light-colored sapwood, typical in cherry (shown) and walnut, isn't considered a defect when grading. You'll just find more of it in No. 1 Common because of the smaller logs.
- **Bad ends.** All it takes to drop a board into No. 1 Common grade is one bad end. Long or numerous checks and clusters of knots that extend more than 12 in. are typical.
- **Warp.** The boards can be bowed, crooked, cupped or twisted, as long as the clear cuttings from them can be planed flat on two sides to the standard surfaced thickness (13/16 in. for 1-in. rough stock, for example).

Knots

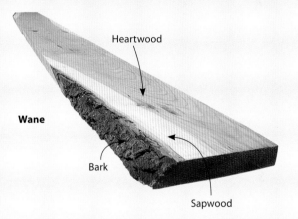

Heartwood

Wane

Bark

Sapwood

Unusable ends

IS CONSTRUCTION LUMBER GOOD FOR FURNITURE?

Q: I've tried to use construction-grade lumber for furniture, but the wood warped like crazy. How can I prevent that?

A: You can't use this wood as it is. You've got to do some selective cutting first and then dry out the wood before making furniture with it.

Construction-grade lumber warps for two main reasons. First, boards often contain unstable wood from the center of the tree. You can spot this by looking at the growth rings at the end of the board. If you see rings that are almost a full circle, that area of the board is likely to cup and twist.

Second, it's too wet. The industry standard for

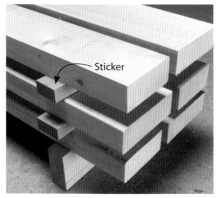

Sticker

Stack and sticker your wood to dry it out before using it for furniture.

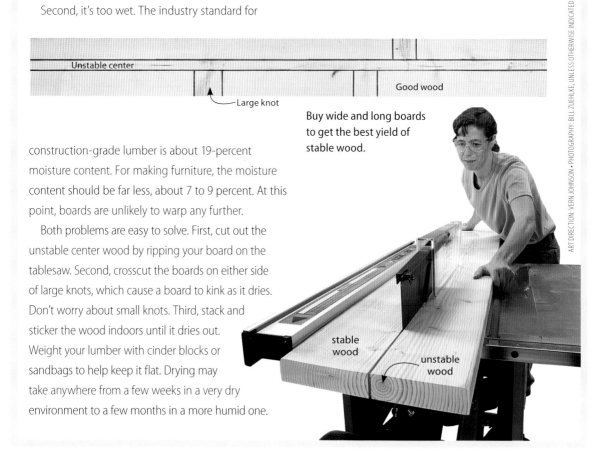

Unstable center

Large knot

Good wood

Buy wide and long boards to get the best yield of stable wood.

stable wood

unstable wood

construction-grade lumber is about 19-percent moisture content. For making furniture, the moisture content should be far less, about 7 to 9 percent. At this point, boards are unlikely to warp any further.

Both problems are easy to solve. First, cut out the unstable center wood by ripping your board on the tablesaw. Second, crosscut the boards on either side of large knots, which cause a board to kink as it dries. Don't worry about small knots. Third, stack and sticker the wood indoors until it dries out. Weight your lumber with cinder blocks or sandbags to help keep it flat. Drying may take anywhere from a few weeks in a very dry environment to a few months in a more humid one.

ART DIRECTION: VERN JOHNSON • PHOTOGRAPHY: BILL ZUEHLKE, UNLESS OTHERWISE INDICATED

Lower Grading Standards For Some Species

Lower grading standards apply to walnut and its close cousin butternut, allowing smaller boards and more defects. And unlike other species, the best side of a walnut board is used to determine its grade. In general, grading rules are tailored to specific species. Walnut trees usually don't get to be giants, so the typical log is undersized. That fact is considered when the boards are graded.

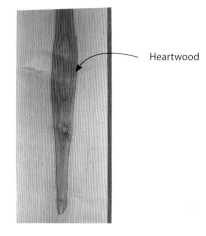

Heartwood

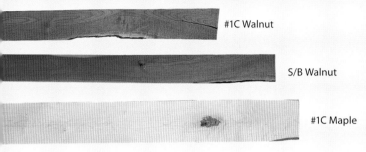

#1C Walnut

S/B Walnut

#1C Maple

Dark-colored heartwood, typical in maple, birch and ash, isn't considered a defect unless the board is also specifically graded for light color. You'll find considerable dark-colored heartwood in No. 1 Common grades of these species, just as you'll find more light-colored sapwood in No. 1 Common cherry and walnut.

Basic Grade Requirements for Hardwoods

The National Hardwood Lumber Association's grading standards are based on the assumption that every board will be cut into defect-free pieces, called "cuttings," for use as furniture components. A board's grade depends on the number and size of the clear pieces it contains. Aesthetics aren't considered.

Grades	Board Size	Minimum Yield of Clear Pieces	Minimum Size Allowed	Maximum Cuttings
Firsts and Seconds (FAS)	6-in. wide x 8-ft. long △	83 to100%	4-in. x 5-ft. or 3-in. x 7-ft.	4
First One Face (F1F)	Same as FAS †	*Each face graded separately: One face must make FAS grade.*		
Selects (SEL)	4-in. wide x 6-ft long	*The second face grades #1C.*		
Selects and Better (SEL/BTR) (combines FAS, F1F and SEL)	4-in. wide x 6-ft long	83 to 100%* 67 to 83%**	4-in. x 5-ft. or 3-in. x 7-ft.* 4-in. x 2-ft. or 3-in. x 3-ft.**	4* 5**
No. 1 Common (#1C)	3-in. wide x 4-ft. long	67 to 83%	4-in. x 2-ft. or 3-in. x 3-ft.	5
No. 2 Common (#2C)	3-in. wide x 4-ft. long	50 to 67%	3-in. x 2-ft.	7
No. 3 Common (#3C)	3-in. wide x 4-ft. long	33 to 50%	3-in. x 2-ft.	unlimited

Best → Worst

△ Smaller boards allowed in some species   * On best face
† Depends on particular species being graded   ** On worst face

Sawing & Milling Great Wood

Few woodworking activities are more satisfying than making something out of boards you've milled yourself. You're free of commercial restraints, and you're able to experiment with unusual species and cuts—including firewood and tree-trimmings that you often can obtain for free. And you can begin with wood that's close to the thickness you want for your project, avoiding a lot of waste and really stretching your wood dollars.

- To become your own sawmill, the key tool you'll need is a well-tuned bandsaw equipped with appropriate shop-made fences and carriages. The bandsaw allows you to slice boards of any thickness out of small and short logs. The only restriction is your own strength: can you lift the log onto the saw table? If so, you'll be able to slice it up into wood you can use.

- Whatever the source, bargain wood is likely to come with all the features that grew in the tree: knots and branch stubs, wildly interlocked grain and fantastic figure where a major limb grew, plus every defect in the lumber-grader's rule book. To make the most of it, you'll need to learn how to read grain direction and how to cope with common defects.

- However you get there, you'll want to end up with boards that are flat in length, uniform in width and thickness, and square in every direction. The advice in this chapter shows you how to read the wood and what to do about its inevitable defects and obstacles.

❮ **Saw it yourself**—*With a highly adjustable shop-made log carriage, you can convert firewood-sized logs into furniture-sized boards and parts. Here's the first cut in progress, breaking the round log into two flat-sided halves.*

JOE GOHMAN

For a Perfect Match, Buy the Whole Log

FOR PERFECTLY MATCHED BOARDS, I ORDERED A WHOLE FLITCH-CUT CHERRY LOG.

I love the look of natural, unstained cherry, but I've never had much luck matching its color and figure. Every cherry board I've bought at a lumberyard has looked different. Some were red; others were brown. Some were curly; others were plain. Variation isn't a big problem with many projects, but when I dived into building a huge dining table, I resolved to be choosy. I wanted showy boards that all looked alike.

Clearly, matched boards must come from the same tree, so I would have to buy from a sawmill or lumber company that keeps all the boards from one log together as a unit, called a flitch. A flitch-cut log is sawn in successive layers (see photo, above) and is dried, stickered and stacked as a unit.

Flitch-cut logs are sold as whole units or in parts. You may have to buy the whole log or you may be able to pick individual boards. Buying a whole log gives you more options in cutting and arranging pieces, but it's also more expensive. You'll probably get more wood than you'll need for a single project.

I turned to the Internet to order my log. That was fun! There are many companies to choose from. On many Web sites, I could see photos of every log and every board in each log. Before I ordered, though, I talked to a real person at the lumberyard who told me more about the log, such as the presence of defects, color, figure and expected yield.

There are as many different logs as there are trees in a forest. I'll tell you a bit about the particular log I ordered, but you shouldn't generalize too much from my experience. First, the price tag. My log cost about $1,000 kiln-dried. Shipping added another $250. That eye-popping price really stretched my budget, but it was worth it. The log was 12 ft. long with center boards 16 in. wide. It was all cut into 1¼-in.-thick (5/4) boards. (Many logs are cut into boards that are 1-in.-thick (4/4) or a mixture of thicknesses.) The log contained 170 bd. ft. of 5/4 wood, which works out to be about $6 per bd. ft.

That's about the same price I pay at the lumberyard for top-grade 5/4 lumber, but the yield of this log was substantially less. Flitch-cut wood generally includes an irregular bark edge, all the sapwood and the pith, which is the soft and unstable center of the tree. It may also contain crotches, where the fork of a branch makes the wood grain much wilder. My log had everything: bark, sapwood, pith and a crotch. The crotch was too highly figured to use in my table, but its grain is so cool that I've set it aside for another project.

My log was sliced into 10 boards. The two outside slices were mostly light-colored sapwood, so I set them aside for use as (expensive) utility wood in other projects. The center four slices were quartersawn and had cracks following the pith. The remaining four slices were plainsawn, wide and relatively defect-free. All in all, my yield was reduced at least 25 percent.

On the plus side, I made eight 12 x 48-in. boards with the same striking figure, two more than I needed. I also cut a lot of 4-in.-wide straight-grained boards (the quartersawn and riftsawn portions of the flitch), which were perfect for the table's aprons.

After all that work, this table really looks fabulous. My spouse knows—all too well— that our table is a real conversation piece. Buying a whole log was an expensive but convenient way to get matched boards. It sure makes a great after-dinner story.

Flitch-cut boards can be expensive, but they make a spectacular top. All the wood matches. Each piece of this cherry dining table has the same golden color and shimmering curly figure.

by GEORGE VONDRISKA

Bandsaw Resawing

CUT LOGS INTO LUMBER, MAKE THIN BOARDS FROM THICK AND CUT YOUR OWN VENEER

Perhaps you want to cut ¾-in.-thick material down to ⅜ in., or make veneer from that one precious figured board. Or maybe you want to get useful lumber from a gorgeous piece of wood in your firewood pile. The technique that makes this possible is resawing. Although it just plain baffles some woodworkers, once you get the hang of it, you'll be surprised at what you can do, even on a small bandsaw. Here's what you need to make it all happen: blade selection, shop-made jigs, setup and cutting tips.

Why Resaw?

One big reason: money. If you want thin stock for small boxes or drawers, it's a lot cheaper to make your own than to buy it. Some wood dealers actually make thin stock by planing down 4/4 material, so it ends up being more expensive to buy less wood!

With wood prices going through the roof, making veneer can stretch your woodworking dollars. Slicing veneer on your bandsaw can change one bd. ft. of precious, expensive wood into six sq. ft. of veneer.

You can also transform those dusty chunks of apple or crotch wood out in your garage into free lumber by resawing. You could make a project entirely from a tree felled in your own yard. Resawing gives you access to the marvelous possibilities of free or cheap local logs.

Blade Selection and More

Just about any bandsaw will do acceptable resawing. For example, all the cuts made in this story were done on an inexpensive, 14-in. bandsaw with a ¾-hp motor. All we did to the saw was add a riser block to increase its capacity. Granted, pushing a saw too hard can bog it down, or even pop a circuit breaker. So take it easy. If you plan to do lots of resawing, see page 45 for more on larger and souped-up machines.

Use the widest blade your saw can handle: ½ in. or ¾ in. for most saws. Wide blades make it easier to cut a straight line. Look for a blade with four teeth per inch and a hook tooth pattern. The hooked teeth give you big gullets (the valleys between the teeth) to clear the sawdust from the cut and help the blade run cool. Heat is a blade's biggest enemy. Resawing pushes your saw's motor to the max, so make it easier on your saw by always using a sharp blade.

I've had perfectly acceptable results resawing with bi-metal blades and great results resawing with silicone-carbide, low-

ART DIRECTION: JOEL SPIES • PHOTOGRAPHY: MIKE HABERMANN • ILLUSTRATION: FRANK ROHRBACH

TIP: If the front of your bandsaw table isn't straight, screw on a strip of hardboard or aluminum bar. This will make it much easier to move and adjust a shop-made fence.

Find the drift angle by drawing a line parallel to one edge of a 16-in.-long scrap piece. Saw the line freehand. Notice how much you have to angle the wood in order to follow a straight line. This is the drift angle.

Stop about halfway through the cut, hold the wood in place and shut off the saw. Trace the angle of the wood onto the bandsaw table.

Set your fence parallel to the line on the table. An adjustable block at the end of the fence allows you to hold this angle as you move the fence laterally. Make sure your table is square to the blade and your fence is square to the table.

Adjustable block

tension blades (see Sources, page 204). These blades leave an excellent surface finish and, due to their thin kerf and low tension, don't take as much power to drive. These blades make it easier to resaw thick stock on any saw.

An auxiliary table helps and is a must for cutting logs. Check out our shop-made table system on page 48. Resawing also requires a fence. Some bandsaw manufacturers have fences available for their saws ($75 to $100), or you can make one (page 48). The fence should be high enough to support the material you're cutting and adjustable to compensate for blade drift.

Don't forget dust collection. Resawing produces lots of dust and it's typically pretty fine. Admittedly, dust collection attachments on most bandsaws aren't great, but whatever you have is better than nothing. If you find lots of dust buildup on your tires, unplug the saw and clean the tires with a rag moistened with mineral spirits. Clean tires help your saw perform better.

Get the Drift: Setup Tips

If you've tried cutting a straight line on your bandsaw, you probably noticed that your material has to be fed at an angle to the blade. This is called "blade drift." Any resaw technique that uses a fence requires finding and working with this drift angle. Drift varies from blade to blade, so follow this simple setup procedure (photo s 1 through 4) every time you change blades.

Set your fence parallel to the line on the table. An adjustable block at the end of the fence allows you to hold this angle as you move the fence laterally. Make sure your table is square to the blade and your fence is square to the table.

Position the fence and resaw your board! Be sure to use a push block and pushstick to keep your fingers well away from the action.

Draw a line down the middle of the log using a pencil and straightedge, or snap a chalk line. With the log secured into the sled, saw the log in half.

Position the fence so the veneer is being cut from the side of the board away from the fence. Although this means moving your fence for each cut, it gives the best results. Use a push block and keep an eye open for the blade blowing out through the face of the veneer. After your first cut, smooth the face of the board with a planer or jointer, and re-position the fence. Repeat until the piece is down to ½-in. thickness. This is about as far as you can safely go.

Set up a fence to resaw the boards. Run one face of your halved log against the fence, and keep going until you've cut the entire log.

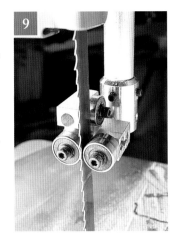

Guide bearings instead of guide blocks (shown here without the guard) can help bandsaw blades run straighter. They cost about $150, and are available for virtually any saw (see Sources, page 204).

Medium-sized bandsaws (16 in. and 18 in.) are excellent for resawing, with larger motors, wider blades and larger tables. Prices are generally $1,000 to $1,800.

Logs to Lumber: Cutting Tips

If your firewood pile puts visions of potential projects into your head, use resawing to turn those logs into planks.

You can cut logs when they're wet or dry, but they'll be easier to cut when wet. Either way, you'll have to dry the lumber all the way before you use it for a project (see "Drying Wood," page 46).

The diameter of the logs you cut is limited by the capacity of your saw: 6 in. on most 14-in. saws. If you want to cut bigger stuff, see if the manufacturer of your saw makes a riser kit. It can increase the capacity of your saw by another 6 in.

Bandsaw Upgrades

For frequent resawing, consider getting a larger saw or souping-up the one you have. You can upgrade to a 1½-hp motor for about $200. At that price, a motor upgrade only makes sense if a slow feed rate is absolutely killing you, or you have to replace the motor for other reasons. Be sure to maintain the same shaft diameter, rpm and rotation direction as your original motor.

Changing your guide blocks to bearing-style guides (photo 9) means investing about $150. The bearings on these guides are designed to run in contact with the blade, eliminating the friction you get from guide blocks. Less friction means less heat and longer blade life. Most of the heat in resawing, however, comes from the blade's contact with the wood. Because bearings can be used in contact with the blade, they can help the blade run straighter, resulting in less drift.

Similarly, nonmetal Cool Blocks ($15) can be run directly against the side of your bandsaw blade. While they won't help the blade run straighter like bearings can, they do make set-up easier. You don't have to worry about spacing the blocks away from the blade.

For increased capacity, look for a riser block ($110) for your saw. These blocks aren't available for all saws, but if you can get one you can increase the saw's capacity by 6 in. They're available for some saws from Delta, Grizzly, Jet, and Ridgid. Riser blocks are saw-specific, so be sure you get the one designed for your saw's specific make and model.

Before dropping too much dough on your bandsaw, remember that $1,000 to $1,800 gets you a brand new saw with big capacity, a monster motor, and guide bearings. These big boys are the ultimate resaw machines.

A bigger table on your saw is almost a must when handling logs. It's nearly impossible to cut a straight line without one. You'll also need a sled to hold onto the log and prevent it from rolling while you cut (below). Once you use the sled, you'll love the stability it gives you for these difficult cuts. Green logs measuring 11 in. in diameter and 36-in. long are about at the top end of what you can safely handle.

Drying Wood

Remember one thing: When it comes to drying, slower is better.

Before cutting the log, paint the end grain. This seals it and slows down the drying process so you don't get lots of cracking. I use whatever extra paint I have around the house, though for green wood, latex is best.

If the bark stays on the planks you cut, leave it on. Like painting the ends, the bark slows down drying.

Stack the planks where air can flow over them, but not in direct sun. Place a couple stickers (1x2s) between each plank so the air can move freely around the wood.

Be patient. Air drying can take as long as one year per inch of thickness. Follow initial drying with a year of storage indoors so the boards equilibrate to indoor moisture levels.

With small planks, use the weighing technique to monitor drying. Weigh the planks after you cut them and use chalk or a marker to record the weight on the wood. Weigh them again every few months. When the weight stops changing, moisture is gone from the wood. Moisture meters are, of course, the most accurate way to gauge the moisture content (see Sources, page 204).

Veneer

Resawing lets you cut your own veneer. This home-sawn veneer has many advantages. It lets you stretch your material by getting lots of sq. ft. out of a single board. Veneering a panel with shop-sawn veneer gives the stability and design options of commercial

Sticker

Sawn and stickered ash from the firewood pile.

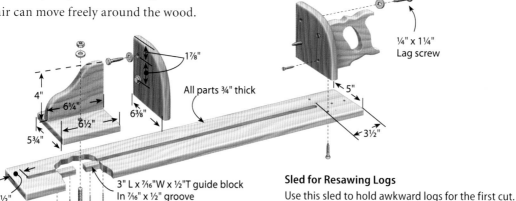

1⅞"

All parts ¾" thick

4"

6¼"

6½"

6⅜"

5¾"

¼" x 1¼"
Lag screw

5"

3½"

3" L x ⁷⁄₁₆"W x ½"T guide block
In ⁷⁄₁₆" x ½" groove

1½"

½" x 1¼"
Carriage bolt

Sled for Resawing Logs
Use this sled to hold awkward logs for the first cut. Hammer the points of the lag screws into the ends of the log to hold it.

Resawn veneer from a precious board of burl.

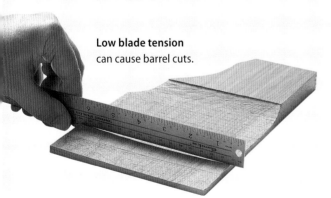

veneer, but with the appearance of solid wood. And because this veneer is thicker than commercial veneer, you can gently round over the edges without cutting into the substrate. You can make veneer from any unusual wood you find, including crotch, spalted, and burled woods—stuff you may not be able to buy from the best veneer supplier. When cutting veneer, always be sure the wood is completely dry before you begin.

A good thickness for your shop-made veneer is ³⁄₃₂ in. It's thick enough to work with, but thin enough to be stable. When sawing, use a fence that's as tall as your material is wide so you have good support, and make sure your fence and blade are perfectly set up. Bandsawn veneer can be edge glued with light clamp pressure.

When Good Cuts Go Bad

So you've mastered the setup, but you're still having problems? Here are some tips:

- Look for these symptoms when you make your test cut: If the board pulls away from the fence on the outfeed side (photo 4), the outfeed end of the fence is angled too far away from the blade. If the board you're cutting binds as you're slicing it, the outfeed end of the fence is angled too close to the blade. Make an adjustment and try another test cut.
- Always use a sharp blade.
- Keep your feed rate slow. Listen to your saw and slow down if it's bogging down.

- Use a blade with the right tooth count. Too many teeth make it hard for the blade to clear the sawdust.
- Even with everything correctly set, your wood may not cooperate. Wood can sometimes be imperfectly dried, and react after it's been cut (photo , right). The only solution is cutting your stock thick enough to plane out the cup after resawing.
- Tension your blade. Too little tension can lead to barrel cuts (photo , left). Check the tension by unplugging the saw, raising the upper guide and pushing on the side of the blade. The blade shouldn't deflect more than ¼ in.

Low blade tension can cause barrel cuts.

Setup for this resaw was perfect, but the wood warped after it was cut. It must now be carefully planed to remove the cup.

SIMPLE LUMBER MAKER

I've turned my bandsaw into a mini sawmill with the help of one dirt-simple jig and a pair of extension tables. The jig is nothing more than a piece of plywood screwed to the log. It steadies the log when I cut the first slab and provides additional support when I rotate the log to saw boards (see photo, below).

My bandsaw is equipped with a fence to guide the jig and a riser block to accommodate the additional height of a log. I use a very coarse ¾-in. 2-tpi blade for sawing thick, green wood. My jig is a piece of ¾-in. plywood 12 in. wide and 6 ft. long. (The largest log the saw and my back can handle is 11 in. dia. and 4 ft. long.)

Attaching the plywood to the log is easy. I just lay the plywood on top of the log and drive 2-in.-long deck screws at three or four points where the board touches the log. (The screws should penetrate at least ½-in. below the bark.) I lift the log onto the extension table and pound some carpenter's shims under both sides of the log to keep it from rocking. The first cut goes through both log and plywood. This creates a flat surface to support the log on its side for the following cuts.

Shim

I flip the plywood jig on its side and ride it against the fence to saw boards. The jig automatically holds the log at a right angle to the first cut I made.

ART DIRECTION: RICK DUPRE AND VERN JOHNSON • PHOTOGRAPHY: PATRICK HUNTER

by TOM CASPAR

Reading Grain Direction

CUT AND PLANE FOLLOWING THE TREE'S STRUCTURE

"Going against the grain" is a familiar phrase. It means doing something the wrong way. When you're talking about wood, you always want to go with the grain—cutting or planing a board in a way that follows the natural structure of the tree (photo 1, page 50). The result is a smooth surface.

How do you figure out which way the grain goes? Some folks use the coin-toss method. They'll joint or plane one side in an arbitrary direction and observe the results. After all, you've got a 50-50 chance of being right! When you're wrong, however, you can be really wrong (photo 2, page 50) and you'll get tear-out.

Whether it's shallow or deep, tear-out means extra work in planing, scraping or sanding a board.

Tear-out will rarely be a problem for you after we show you how to read the fibers inside a board. Most woodworkers think that the ovals or lines on the surface of a board are the key to grain direction, but this type of "grain" is not completely reliable for predicting fiber direction (photo 3, page 51). Going with the grain really means going with the fibers. In the pages to follow, we'll show you other clues that are more dependable in predicting the fiber direction in hardwoods.

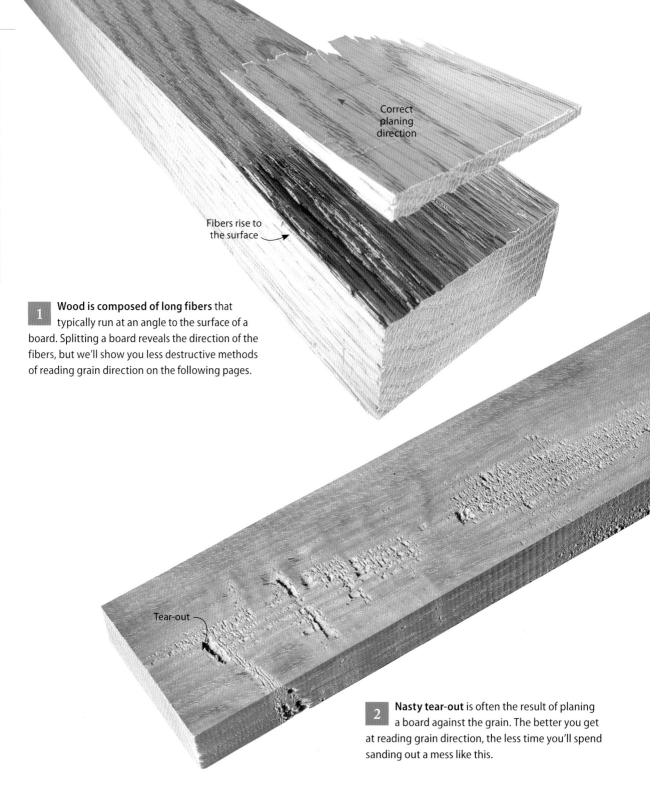

Correct planing direction

Fibers rise to the surface

1 **Wood is composed of long fibers** that typically run at an angle to the surface of a board. Splitting a board reveals the direction of the fibers, but we'll show you less destructive methods of reading grain direction on the following pages.

Tear-out

2 **Nasty tear-out** is often the result of planing a board against the grain. The better you get at reading grain direction, the less time you'll spend sanding out a mess like this.

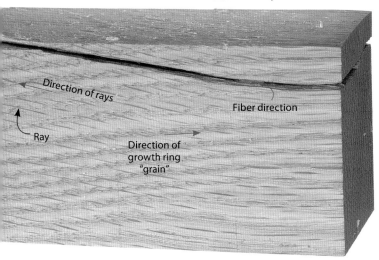

Plane this way ←

Direction of rays ←

Ray

Direction of growth ring "grain"

Fiber direction

3 **Grain direction can fool you.** Normally we call patterns of ovals and lines made by the growth rings the "grain" of the wood. We assume that the fiber direction runs the same way. The split-off piece of red oak at right shows that this "grain" and the fiber direction don't necessarily go the same way. Small cells called rays are the true indicators of fiber direction in plainsawn oak. (Plainsawn boards are also commonly called flatsawn boards. See page 52 for more information on rays and plainsawn boards.)

4 **Feel the fuzz on rough lumber.** No kidding, you can tell which way to plane rough lumber merely by running your hand over it! The direction that the fibers go feels smooth, while the opposite direction feels rough and jagged. That's because many individual fibers actually stick out above the surface of rough lumber. You're feeling their sharp ends.

5 **Know where to look.** On smooth lumber, the clues to fiber direction are on the surface of the wood.

You can't read fiber direction just by looking at the surface you want to plane, however. The clues to look for are on the edge adjacent to the surface you'll plane. To plane the top (1), look at the side (2). To plane the side, look at the top.

What are Rays?

Ray cells radiate from the center of a tree. These long, thin ribbons show different faces depending on how the board is cut from the tree.

You can clearly see the wide side of the rays when the surface of a board runs at a right angle to the growth rings. This surface is called a quartersawn or radial face, and the ray's wide sides are called ray fleck.

When the surface of a board runs more or less parallel to the growth rings, you only see the narrow ends of the rays. This is how most boards are sawn, and this surface is called a plainsawn, flatsawn or tangential face.

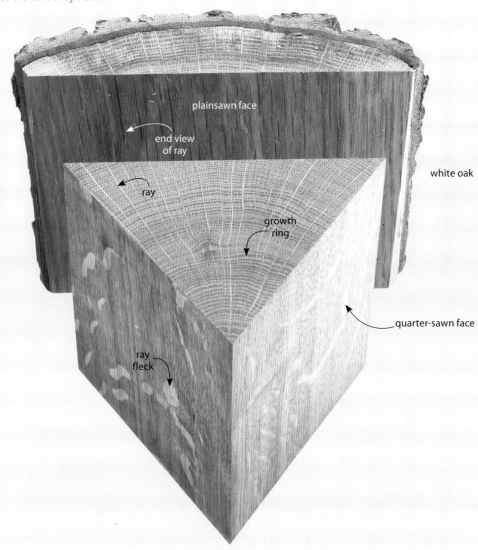

plainsawn face

end view of ray

ray

growth ring

white oak

quarter-sawn face

ray fleck

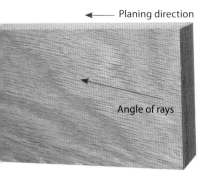

← Planing direction

Angle of rays

6 **Rays are the best clues** to fiber direction in hardwoods. The general angle of the rays on the plainsawn face of a board invariably point in the same direction as the wood's fibers. This typical piece of red oak is easy to read because oak's rays are quite prominent. Beech and sycamore also have large rays. Cherry, maple and many other woods have rays that are paler and much smaller, but you can find them if you look closely. Some hardwoods, such as ash and walnut, have rays that are too small to see.

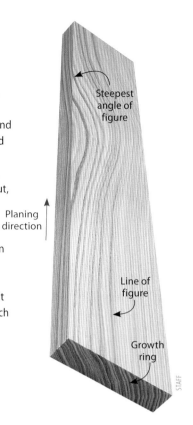

Steepest angle of figure

Planing direction ↑

Line of figure

Growth ring

STAFF

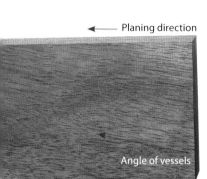

← Planing direction

Angle of vessels

7 **Look for vessels** to indicate fiber direction when you can't see rays. Vessels are cells that look like long, dark dashes. They're easy to spot on this piece of walnut once you know what you're looking for. Mahogany, butternut and birch also have clearly visible vessel cells, as do many other woods.

← Planing direction

Angle of figure

8 **Figure is a last resort.** If you can't see rays or vessels, go with the angle of the dark lines that most woodworkers call the "grain" of a board. ("Figure" is the more accurate term.) We're all familiar with the concentric growth rings on the end of a board (photo 9). If you follow those rings around to the face or edge, they become the lines and ovals that lend each board a distinctive figure.

9 **Fiber direction can often run two ways.** Tear-out may be inevitable no matter which way you plane this board, but you can minimize it using the clues to fiber direction given here. In this piece of ash, the figure made by the growth rings is the only obvious clue to follow. The angle of this figure is steeper at one end of the board than the other. Always use the steeper end to decide which way to plane.

Planing direction

10 **Mark fiber direction** on the end of the board. This mark means "begin planing the top surface here." It can't be accidentally removed as you mill the faces or edges of your lumber.

by TOM CASPAR

5 Steps to Foursquare Boards

STRAIGHT, FLAT, AND SQUARE

I t sounds obvious, but the key to accurate woodworking is to start with accurately machined boards. They must be straight, flat, and square. Roughsawn lumber is anything but. Here's a time-honored order of procedure to turn rough boards into foursquare boards.

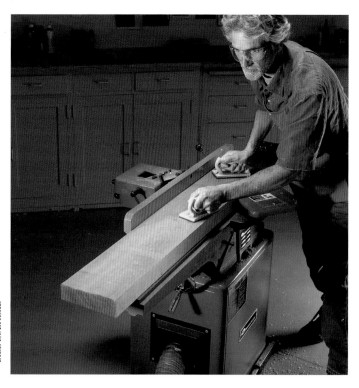

BILL ZUEHLKE

RAMON MORENO

ART DIRECTION: VERN JOHNSON • PHOTOGRAPHY: VERN JOHNSON, UNLESS NOTED

Joint One Face:
Make one face flat and smooth using your jointer. It's OK to leave some low spots here and there. If you get tear-out, try feeding from the opposite end. Mark the feed direction that gives the best results on the end of the board. This mark indicates grain direction and reminds you to "start here."

"Start here" mark

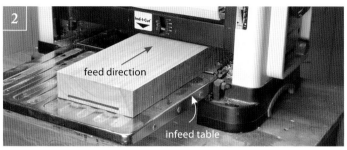

feed direction

infeed table

Plane the Opposite Side:
Use your thickness planer to make the other rough face parallel to the jointed face. Grain direction is easy to figure out: The grain on the second face runs in the opposite direction as the grain on the first face. That means the mark you made in Step 1 should appear on the end nearest you, face down, as you feed each board into the planer.

Joint One Edge:
Make one edge flat, straight and square. Grain direction matters here, too. If you get tear-out going one direction, turn the board around, place the opposite face against the jointer's fence and try again. This is the reason you thickness-plane before you edge-joint: If you only have one smooth face, you could only edge-joint in one direction.

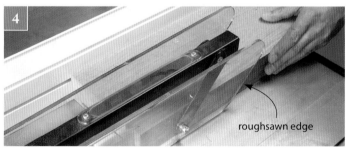

roughsawn edge

Rip the Opposite Edge:
Use your tablesaw to cut a second edge parallel to the first. Make the cut about $\frac{1}{32}$ in. wider than the final dimension. Then return to the jointer and make a $\frac{1}{32}$-in.-deep cut on the ripped edge. Now both edges are smooth and square to the board's faces.

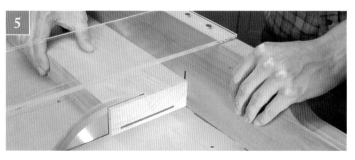

Crosscut the Ends:
Use your tablesaw or miter saw to square one end of the board. Then use a stop block to cut it to length.

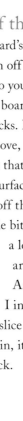

by TOM CASPAR

8 Tips for Milling Rough Lumber

GET THE BEST YIELD FROM THE LEAST-EXPENSIVE WOOD

Transforming a long, gnarly plank of rough lumber into a set of perfectly milled boards is immensely satisfying. Not only do you save money, but you become intimate with the character of every precious piece of wood. The biggest benefit, however, is being absolutely certain that your boards are truly flat, straight and square. That's the solid foundation you need to make accurate cuts, lay out precise joints and glue boards together without gaps. Here are some helpful pointers to build that foundation.

⌄ Cut Off the Ends First

Cracks in a board's ends are a common flaw. Cut them off before you do any other crosscutting, so you know the true, usable length of your board. These cracks are also called end checks. Large checks are easy to see and remove, but you may also find hairline cracks that aren't easily visible on the board's surface or end.

I cut off the end of a board a little bit at a time, like slicing a loaf of bread. The slices are about ¼ in. thick. As each slice falls off, I inspect it for checks. If the slice breaks very easily across the grain, it probably contains a hairline check.

Check

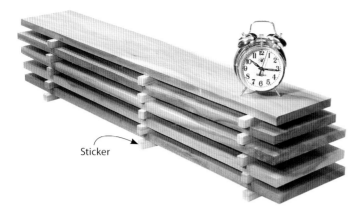

Sticker

⌃ Let Boards Rest

To make pieces dead flat, I usually let boards rest before taking them down to final thickness. I plane boards ⅛ in. thicker than needed and stack them with stickers or stand them on edge so air can circulate around every side.

After the boards rest for a day or so, I check each board for flatness by laying it on my tablesaw or jointer. It's not unusual to find that some previously flat boards have cupped or twisted a bit. I rejoint one side of these boards, then plane every board to final thickness.

⟩ Cut Big Boards into Small Pieces

You might think the best strategy for milling rough lumber is to flatten as large a piece as possible, then cut it into smaller parts. Not true. It's better to cut a big roughsawn board into individual pieces, one for each part on your cutting list, more or less, and then start milling. Cut oversize by ½ in. of length and ¼ in. of width.

The problem with the big-board strategy is that the smaller pieces may not end up flat or straight. Some boards have a lot of internal stress. When the board is whole, all this stress is in balance. When you rip the board, you release some of that stress. Each piece seeks a new balance and a new shape. A flat, straight board ripped down the middle might well make two boards that aren't flat or straight. It's hard to predict which boards will react this way.

Chalk line

ART DIRECTION: VERN JOHNSON • PHOTOGRAPHY: RAMON MORENO, UNLESS NOTED

› Follow the Grain

I'm sure you've seen boards like the one at right whose grain runs off the edge in a bad way. If that board becomes part of a project, its slanting grain stands out like a sore thumb. I prefer to eliminate this problem at the outset, while the board is still rough. When I've got this type of board, and enough width to spare, I cut a new edge that more truly follows the grain.

I prefer to use the bandsaw for ripping rough lumber, but a circular saw works well, too. If you're ripping long boards on the bandsaw, use a tall support on the outfeed side to steady the workpiece.

⌄ Mark Grain Direction

As I'm jointing the faces of rough boards, I always mark grain direction on the board's end. This mark tells me to "start the cut here" on the nearest face. This line won't be removed by jointing or planing.

When I stack boards for planing, I look at the marks and orient them all the same way: face down and pointing away from the planer (see "5 Steps to Foursquare Boards," page 54). Even if the boards fall onto the floor as they come out of the machine, I can easily reassemble them with the grain all going the same way, and get right back to work.

VERN JOHNSON

Partially planed surface

Skip Plane To Reveal Grain

What exactly is under that rough surface? Sometimes it's quite difficult to read the grain, spot defects or figure out where the sapwood lies in a roughsawn board— all the things you'd want to know before cutting it up.

If I'm stumped, I run the whole board through the planer. I plane just enough to remove the high spots and skip over the low spots. I don't need to see an entirely planed surface to mark up the board for cutting into smaller pieces.

When the board comes out of the planer, I don't assume it's flat. I'll cut it up into smaller pieces and joint one face of every piece before running it through the planer again. You lose a bit of the board's maximum thickness when you skip plane, but that's usually no big deal.

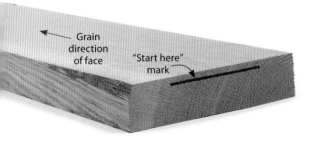

Grain direction of face

"Start here" mark

‹ Avoid Badly Twisted Boards

Some twisted boards are hopeless causes. You might just as well turn them into firewood. Sure, you can joint them flat, but a few rogue boards have a nasty habit of slowly continuing to twist, no matter how many times they're jointed or how short or narrow you cut them.

If your rough lumber is only slightly twisted, however, don't get too alarmed. It doesn't mean you've got junk wood. It may remain perfectly stable after it's milled. Just cut it as short and narrow as you can in the rough state—but not less than 12 in. long—to get the maximum yield in thickness.

⌄ Use the Best Crosscutting Tools

Rough lumber can be tricky to crosscut safely. Its faces and edges are rarely flat and straight, so using a chop saw, miter saw or tablesaw is not the best practice, because the blade could bind, stall, or kick back.

My favorite tools for crosscutting are a jigsaw, a circular saw, and a Japanese tree-trimming saw. This very coarse handsaw cuts incredibly fast, even through thick hardwoods.

I generally crosscut before doing any jointing or planing. Crosscutting reduces a big board to more manageable sizes, so I can mill more accurately. I put my board on four sawhorses for plenty of support and mark it with chalk, a felt-tip pen, or a carpenter's soft-leaded pencil.

by TOM CASPAR

Knots

KNOTTY BOARDS ARE BEAUTIFUL, YET FRUSTRATING! HERE'S HOW TO GET THE MOST OUT OF THEM.

Knots are usually considered defects in wood. They're cut out of boards and thrown on a scrap heap. But take a closer look at a knot. In a hardwood, it's surrounded by stunning grain. Why not make it the focal point of your next project?

The best knots crop up on some of the least expensive, lowest grade boards available. Dealing with knots can add extra work to a project, but you don't need any special equipment. You just have to know what you're up against. To begin, take a look at where the three basic types of knots come from in the photos at right.

growth ring

‹ An intergrown knot is the base of a living branch within a tree. It's surrounded by a halo of circular growth rings. An intergrown knot is also called a "tight" knot because it's tightly bound to the wood around it.

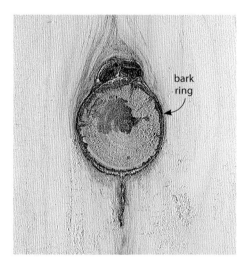

bark ring

‹ An encased knot is formed when a tree grows around a dead branch. It's surrounded by a dark ring of bark, and its center is often decayed. An encased knot is also called a "loose" knot, because the bark prevents the knot from tightly binding to the wood around it.

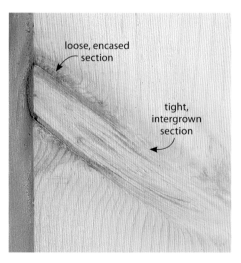

loose, encased section

tight, intergrown section

‹ A spike knot is formed when a board is cut right through the length of a branch. A spike knot may be tight at its base (the intergrown portion) and loose at its end (the encased portion).

spike
knot

intergrown
knot

› Use knots for drama.

Here's an opportunity to have
fun with unusual patterns, as in this
spalted-maple kitchen table. It has a
comet-shaped pairing of a huge intergrown
knot and a very long spike knot. Showing off
the incredible swirling grain around a knot
turns an inexpensive, lower grade board into
a beautiful example of nature's art..

‹ Resawing can be spectacular!

A board with knots near an edge yields the
most interesting mirror-image patterns, as
shown in this piece of aromatic red cedar.
Before you cut a board down its length on
a bandsaw, hold the board on edge against
a mirror. The outside of the board and its
reflected image give you a pretty good
idea of the book-matched pattern you'll
get after resawing.

‹ Pound out an encased knot before ripping a board on the tablesaw. If a saw blade were to catch this knot, it would launch it like a missile! The best tool to drive out a knot is a large dowel, rather than a slender metal punch. A punch can get stuck inside a decayed knot, but the wide end of a dowel pushes the whole knot through. Taper the dowel so its end is about the same diameter as the knot.

‹ Glue a loose knot that you want to keep with 5-minute epoxy. Epoxy is the only type of glue that can span the gaps between the knot and the solid wood around it. Scrape off loose bark around the knot and inside the hole before gluing.

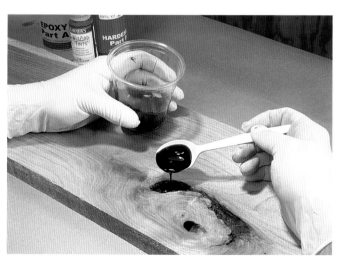

‹ Fill voids around a knot with slow-set epoxy. Color the epoxy with a few drops of dark concentrated dye (see Sources, page 204). Slow-set is better than fast-set epoxy for this use. Slow-set epoxy takes a few hours to harden, so unsightly air bubbles have a chance to rise to the top and pop rather than get trapped inside. Mix the epoxy and dye very slowly to minimize the number of bubbles. Slightly overfill the hole and sand the hardened epoxy flush.

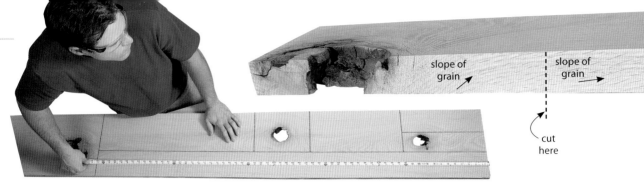

slope of grain →

slope of grain →

cut here

∧ Keep your distance from knots when you're cutting them out. It's tempting to get the last inch out of every clear piece, but often it's not worth it. The wood fibers around a knot have a very steep slope. (Right next to the knot, they run almost vertically, the same direction as the branch grew on the tree.) Wood fibers with a steep slope are called "short grain." Short grain weakens the end of a board, making it unsuitable for rails and legs. Short grain may also cause the end to chip out when you joint or plane the board.

⌄ A knot near the edge can cause a sharp bend or "kink" in a board. The wood around a knot is under an incredible amount of stress caused by supporting the weight of a branch. The stress is balanced when the knot is in the middle of a board, and unbalanced when the knot is near the edge. Kinks are trouble, so they're a good place to crosscut a board.

⌄ A knot near a glue line may eventually cause the glue line to open up or the boards to become uneven. The extreme slope of the grain around a knot is the culprit. It causes the wood around a knot to expand and contract differently than the wood in the rest of a board.

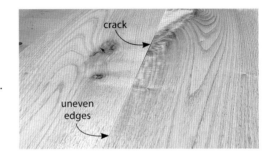

crack

uneven edges

Knots can be so beautiful that it would be a shame never to make a top like this, however. A little unevenness is perfectly acceptable in many fine antiques, after all!

Here's a tip for building a new piece: When you join boards in a top with knots near the edges, rout a ⅛-in.-deep V-groove down the center of all the glue joints. This will disguise any small cracks or unevenness that may crop up later.

kink

⌃ Avoid placing a knot in a slender piece. For example, a knot weakens this leg and may eventually cause it to kink. The small knot on this table's rail shouldn't cause any distortion problems, however. It's surrounded by a great deal of straight-grained wood. The knot can be hidden from sight by rounding over the edge.

⌄ Wide boards with large knots are generally free of distortion problems, as long as the knots are located in the middle and far enough from the ends. The stresses inside the wood around the knot are balanced, so the boards are unlikely to kink. The ends of the boards are plenty strong, and there are no uneven glue joints to worry about. Piles of 10- to 14-in.-wide lower grade wood often have beautiful knotty boards waiting to be discovered.

⌃ Seal knots with dewaxed shellac before applying a top coat. Brush on two coats of a two-pound cut. Without this seal coat, small bubbles may appear in your finish above the knots. The bubbles are called "bleed-through," and they're caused by oils in the knots reacting with the finish. Pine knots are the worst offenders. Shellac is the most effective barrier to these oils. When its wax has been removed, shellac can be used under any finish.

by D A V E   M U N K I T T R I C K

Recipe for Resawing

AMAZING WOOD AT FANTASTIC PRICES HARVESTED CLOSE TO HOME

For a woodworker, few things are more satisfying than resawing thin sheets of veneer off of a large block of wood or slicing a beautiful board in half to create two bookmatched pieces. I remember the enthusiasm I felt when I tried resawing for the first time. My excitement soon turned to disappointment however, as I watched my bandsaw chew up piece after piece of expensive walnut. Grrrrrr. It took me a long time to get over that initial experience. There's no reason for you to share my pain, though. Here's a recipe that will give you great results every time you resaw.

1 **Choose the Right Blade.** The single most important key to success is to use a sharp, high-quality blade. A dull blade is nothing but trouble. Here's what to look for: First, use as wide a blade as your saw can handle. That said, we don't recommend using a ¾-in. blade on a 14-in. bandsaw unless the blade thickness is no more than .025 in.

Second, choose a blade with three to four teeth per inch (tpi) and a 5- to 10-degree hook. Coarse blades have deeper gullets for better sawdust clearance. The hook tooth is an aggressive cutting design that lessens the feed pressure required. Reduced feed pressure keeps the blade from deflecting, which results in a straighter cut.

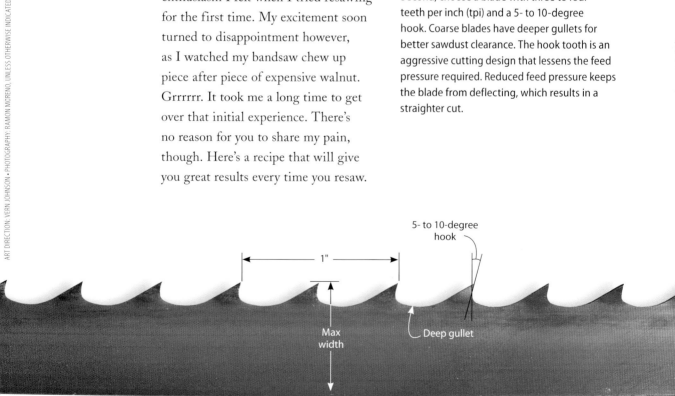

1"

Max width

5- to 10-degree hook

Deep gullet

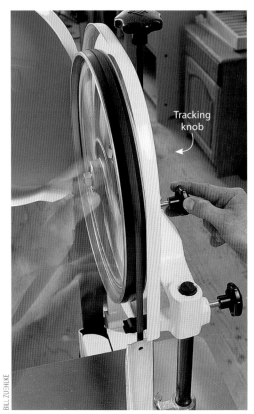

Caution! Blade guard retracted for this step. Be careful.

2 **Adjust Tracking.** With the saw unplugged, back off the thrust bearings and guides as far as possible. Mount the blade and temporarily set the tension according to the gauge on the saw. Manually spin the upper wheel and adjust the tracking knob until the blade is more or less centered on the wheel.

3 **Set Blade Tension.** The flutter test is the best way I've found to set the tension on a bandsaw blade. Keep the guides and bearings backed off and raise the blade guard to the maximum height. Stand clear of the blade and turn the machine on. Decrease the blade tension until the blade begins to flutter back and forth. Now, increase the tension until the blade flutter is eliminated. Add a one-half turn or so to the tension knob and the blade tension should be just right.

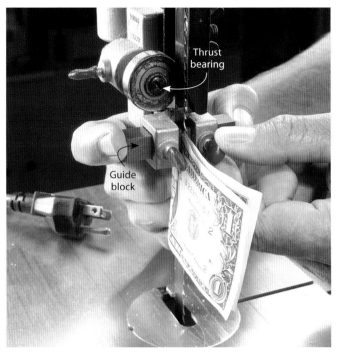

Thrust bearing

Guide block

4 **Adjust the Guides.** I use the thickness of a dollar bill or a piece of paper as a spacer for setting the guide blocks and thrust bearings. First, set the blade guide arm so it's about ¼ in. above the height of the stock you're resawing. Then bring the guide block assembly forward until the fronts of the blocks are even with the bottoms of the blade gullets. Wrap a dollar bill around the blade and set the blocks up tight against the sides of the blade. Use the bill again to set the thrust bearing behind the blade. Repeat the process for the lower guide blocks and thrust bearing. Non-metallic blocks, such as Cool Blocks, can be set in direct contact with the blade and don't need the dollar bill spacer.

Scrap

5 **Find the Drift Angle.** Try cutting a straight line on your bandsaw. You'll notice that your stock has to be fed at an angle in order to make a straight cut. This is called the "drift angle."

Setting the fence at the right drift angle is critical to successful resawing. Start by cutting a straight line on a piece of scrap. Stop the cut about half way and trace the angle of the board onto the bandsaw table. This represents the angle your fence needs to be set at in order to make a straight cut. Set your fence parallel to the line on the table and you're ready to resaw. Try a test cut first. Most of the time, everything works great right off the bat. Occasionally, I find a few minor adjustments to the fence angle or a little more tension is required for best performance.

Finally, be sure your stock is jointed square and that your blade is square to your table and don't forget to use push sticks at the end of the cut.

Drying Your Own Wood

O nce you've made logs into boards, whether by doing it yourself or by purchasing green lumber from a small sawmill, you've got to dry the wood before you'll be able to use it. The cost of drying is a significant portion of the price of commercial wood. By doing it yourself, you can save that money. But because it is wood, it shrinks as it dries, and if you dry it too quickly or incorrectly, you'll end up with firewood instead of useful material. The process is called seasoning; it takes a while, and there are three basic approaches the individual woodworker can take.

- You can air-dry the wood outdoors under cover. This is the simplest, time-tested approach. The main thing is to build the wood pile carefully, with spacers called stickers separating the layers of wood and allowing air to circulate. Then you just wait.

- You can build a simple indoor kiln based upon a household dehumidifier and a fan. The kiln is just a box, the dehumidifier allows you to control the humidity inside it, and the fan drives the drying air over the stickered boards. By slowly lowering the humidity, you'll slowly dry the wood.

- You can build a shed-like outdoor kiln that uses the sun's energy to dry the wood.

- Whatever wood-drying solution you choose, you will need a way to accurately measure the wood's moisture content. This section includes a roundup of inexpensive moisture meters to take all the guesswork out of the process.

❮ **Dry it Yourself**—*What could be happier for the woodworker than an endless stash of perfectly seasoned and ready-to-work wood that comes out of your own drying kiln? With a home-built box in a corner of the basement, this dude's got it made.*

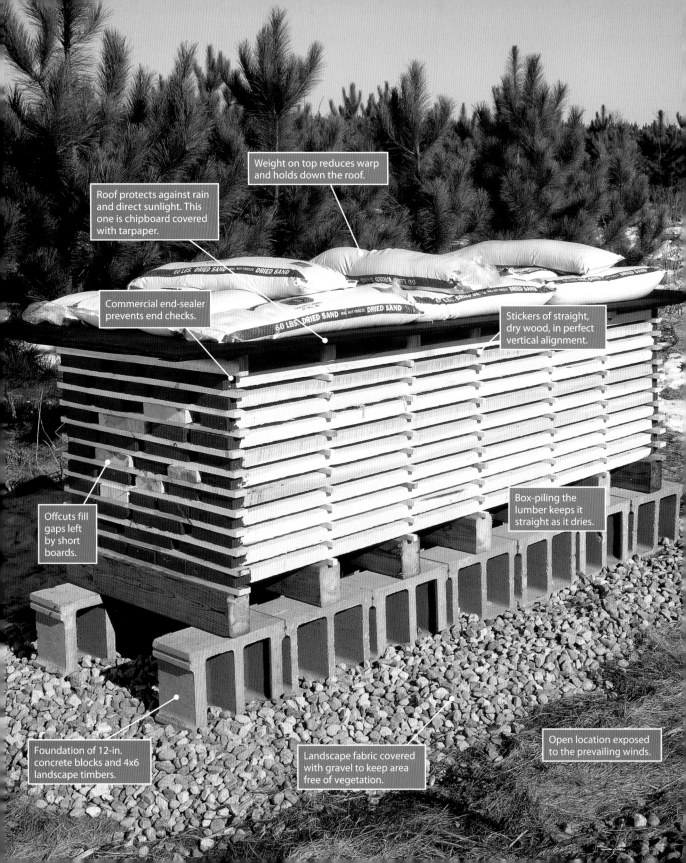

Weight on top reduces warp and holds down the roof.

Roof protects against rain and direct sunlight. This one is chipboard covered with tarpaper.

Commercial end-sealer prevents end checks.

Stickers of straight, dry wood, in perfect vertical alignment.

Offcuts fill gaps left by short boards.

Box-piling the lumber keeps it straight as it dries.

Foundation of 12-in. concrete blocks and 4x6 landscape timbers.

Landscape fabric covered with gravel to keep area free of vegetation.

Open location exposed to the prevailing winds.

by DAVE MUNKITTRICK

Air-Drying Lumber

IT'S THE LOW-COST, LOW-TECH WAY TO DRY LUMBER. HERE'S HOW TO DO IT RIGHT

Want a truly cheap and easy way to dry lumber? Consider air drying. It's the most economical method for removing water from wood, and when done properly, you'll end up with perfect lumber.

Although air-drying is inexpensive and easy, be aware of these drawbacks:

- It's slow. Depending on the species and your climate, it can take from 2 to 12 months to bring 4/4 lumber from green to air-dry (12- to 20-percent moisture content, depending on your location).
- Air-dry isn't dry enough for indoor use. If you're planning to use the lumber for outdoor projects, air-drying outdoors is fine. But if you plan to use the lumber for interior projects, you'll have to re-stack it indoors and let it dry down to 6- to 8-percent moisture content.
- Loss of material. When you air-dry lumber, it's not unusual to lose up to 10 percent or more to drying defects. Lumber defects occur when drying is too rapid, which leads to surface checks and end splits or when drying is too slow, which results in sticker stains and discoloration from fungal growth. Because air-drying is at the mercy of the weather, drying rates are difficult to control.

There's not much you can do about the slowness or the final moisture content, but you can ensure that your lumber has the fewest possible drying defects. It's all in how you stack the pile. Here's how to do it right.

Put Your Pile in the Open

Locate the stack in an open area exposed to the prevailing winds. Avoid shady spots or low areas where moisture can collect on the ground.

Keep the area around the stack clean and free of vegetation. Debris from off-cuts or broken stickers and sawdust are breeding grounds for insects that can migrate to your stack. Control vegetation around an outdoor pile by laying down landscape cloth and covering it with gravel.

Box-piled lumber yields the most high-quality boards.
The pile should have:
- Straight sides and ends
- Full-length boards on the outside of the pile
- Short boards staggered through the inside of the pile
- Offcuts used as spacers to bridge the gaps caused by short boards.

(image labels: Spacer, Short Board)

Prepare a Good Foundation

For outdoor drying, the foundation should be at least 18-in. high. We used 12-in. cement blocks and 4x6 landscape timbers to keep the bottom of the pile up off the moist ground and to encourage airflow through the bottom of the stack. Level the cement blocks to create a flat foundation. A dip in the foundation will telegraph through your whole stack resulting in less-than-flat boards. Place the timbers on 16-in. centers.

Prepare the Boards for Stacking

First, trim the ends of the boards so they are a uniform length. Be especially careful to remove any existing checks, because they'll only increase during the drying process.

Then, "butter" the ends with a commercial end-sealer (see Sources, page 204). The money you spend on end-sealer will be more than paid back in better quality lumber. Make sure the coating is thick enough to indent with your fingernail.

You may find some variance in the thickness of your green stock. Sort your wood so that all the boards in a layer are within 1/16-in. of the same thickness.

Use Good-Quality Stickers

Stickers create gaps between the layers of wood. These gaps allow air to flow freely through the stack. Make your stickers from dried wood. They should be straight-grained and strong, so they can be used over and over again. Standard stickers should be surfaced to a uniform ¾ in. x ¾ in. Use 2- to 3-in.-wide stickers at the ends of the stack. The extra width helps slow the rapid loss of moisture at the ends of the boards and makes the stack more stable. Stickers should be slightly longer than the overall width of the stack. It is essential that each sticker be placed directly in line with the one below. This creates a vertical column that transfers all the weight of the stack to the foundation.

Box-Pile the Stack

"Box-piling" is the best way to build your drying stack (photo 1, page 74). In box-piling, full-length boards are used on the outside edges, and shorter boards are placed in the interior of the stack. Fill the voids at the ends of the pile with offcuts from trimming.

Put a Lid on It

If your stack is outside, it needs a roof to keep out damaging direct sunlight and rain. You don't need anything fancy, although it's good to have a slight slope in the roof for water run-off (left) We used chipboard covered with tar-paper. It's best if the roof overhangs the pile by 6 in. or more.

Weight the Stack

Weight (rocks, cement blocks, sandbags) will lock the boards in place, helping to prevent warp and twist as they dry. Plus, it keeps the roof from blowing away.

Control the Wind

To help minimize the effects of the weather, it's best to have a tarp that can be dropped down the sides of the pile. This offers protection on hot windy days when the drying rate can be too rapid. This is important with hard-to-dry, check-prone woods like oak and hickory, especially when the green wood is above 30 percent moisture content.

After you've done all you can to protect the quality of your air-dried lumber, it's up to nature.

Tall Sticker

Short Sticker

A slanted roof helps the pile shed water. You can do this in a number of ways; here we are using stickers on the top that vary in height to slant the roof to one end of the pile.

by DAVE MUNKITTRICK

Moisture Meters

STOP GUESSING WHETHER YOUR WOOD IS TOO WET

Think of a moisture meter as cheap insurance. Spend $70 and you'll never have to wonder whether that lumber you bought is too wet or too dry. You can tell if the "kiln-dried" pine you bought from the home center was dried to 9- percent moisture content (about what you need for indoor projects) or 19-percent (what most construction-grade pine is kiln dried to). Knowing the moisture content (MC) of your wood helps you determine when the wood is stable enough to use.

Pin vs. Pinless Meters

How They Work

There are two types of meters on the market, pin and pinless. Both types of meters measure the effect of moisture on an electric current (pin type) or an electromagnetic field (pinless) to determine the moisture content (MC) of the wood (photo 1, page 78). The beauty of a pinless meter is that it can quickly scan an entire board without putting holes in the wood. You can even take it to the lumberyard to test the wood before you buy; try that with a pin meter! One concern about pinless meters is that the sensor pad must be in good contact with the wood for accurate readings. Very rough or warped stock may leave too many air pockets under the sensor pad. I've found a few swipes with a block plane creates a nice flat spot to take your readings.

Pin meters can take readings in wood no matter what the shape, size or degree of roughness. All that's required is that the two pins make contact with the wood. Pin meters also allow you to use remote probes (photo 2, page 78). Nails or probes can be driven to the center of thick lumber for core readings that are out of reach for pinless meters. If you dry your own wood, the probes can be left in a sample board in the stack to monitor the wood as it dries. Plus, pin meters can take readings on the edge of a board stacked for drying (photo 3, page 79).

Species and Temperature Correction

Temperature and wood density affect the readings given by moisture meters. All meters are calibrated to read the MC of Douglas fir at about 68 degrees F. (The Timber Check is the only exception; it is calibrated for red oak). That means if you're using a meter on something other than Douglas fir and the temperature is above or below 68 degrees F, you'll need to make adjustments to the meter reading. Manufacturers include charts that adjust for species and temperature variations. More expensive meters have built-in species correction and a couple have built-in temperature correction as well (see chart page 97). Just set the meter to the desired species and the meter automatically corrects the readings. This is a huge benefit when you have a lot of wood to test.

Pin meters are more sensitive to temperature variations than pinless meters. That's why pin meters always come with temperature correction charts. Some manufacturers include corrections for pinless meters should you need a very precise reading.

Pinless meters, on the other hand, are more sensitive to differences in density, or "specific gravity" of different species than pin meters. That's why pin meters with built-in species correction can get away with grouping species into a handful of settings while pinless meters generally require you to set the specific gravity of each species into the meter.

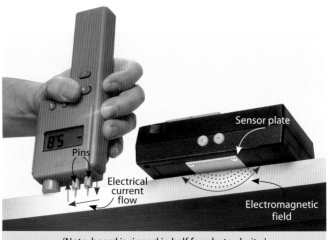

(Note: board is ripped in half for photo clarity.)

1 **Pin and pinless meters measure moisture differently.** Pin meters have a pair of nail-like probes that are inserted into the wood. An electric current is sent between the two pins. Because water is a good conductor of electricity and wood is a poor conductor, the meter can tell how much water is in the wood by how much current travels between the pins.

A pinless meter has a sensor plate that's held against the surface of the wood. The plate projects an electrical field into the wood. The meter can sense changes in the field caused by moisture and wood. The meter then converts the change to a moisture content reading.

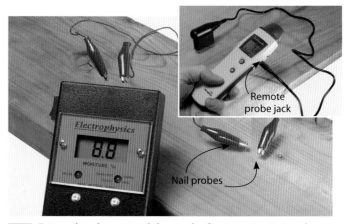

2 **External probes extend the reach of your meter.** External probes driven to the center of a board allow you to get a core reading in stock that's too thick for the pins built into the meter. The probes can also be left in a stack of green wood where readings can be taken to monitor the wood as it dries. Some meters have built-in jacks for aftermarket probes, but a pair of nails and alligator clips are an effective, low-cost alternative for all pin-type meters.

3 **Taking readings from the edges of boards in a stack is a task better suited to pin meters.** Most pinless meters have sensing plates that are too big to read the edge of a 4/4 board.

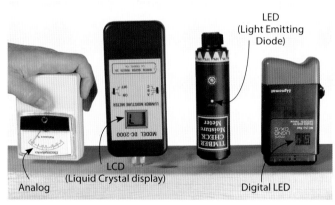

LED
(Light Emitting Diode)

LCD
(Liquid Crystal display)

Analog

Digital LED

4 **Four types of displays are available on moisture meters.** We liked the digital LED and LCD displays the best. Analog displays are the hardest to read. LCD models show the moisture content value on a little screen. This type of display is easy to read in full sun but hard to read in dim light. LED models turn on when the right moisture setting is dialed in on the meter. With a digital LED, the numbers themselves light up. A digital LED is easy to read in the dim light of a storage shed, but difficult to see in full sun.

Should I Buy a Pin or Pinless Meter?

That's the first question everyone asks when looking to buy a moisture meter. The question is best answered by identifying what you want a meter for and comparing that need to the advantages unique to each type of meter.

If you tend to buy surfaced stock and can't bear the thought of poking holes in expensive lumber, then a pinless meter is probably your best bet.

If you buy rough stock, dry your own wood, use wood thicker than 2 in. or have a weakness for piles of rough lumber discovered in some old barn, a pin meter is for you.

Important Features

Pin Length

A rule of thumb states that the average MC of a board can be found at a depth equal to $\frac{1}{15}$ to $\frac{1}{4}$ the thickness of the board. For example, $\frac{5}{16}$-in. 5 pins are long enough to get an average MC reading on a 1½-in.-thick board and ½-in. pins will work for 2-in. stock. Remember, however, that this rule works only when the board has an even moisture gradient where the surface is drier than the core.

It's tempting to think that a pin meter measures the MC of the wood at the ends of the pins. In reality, the uninsulated pins measure the wettest layer of wood they come in contact with. Wood that's been stored in a shed or shop can have a higher MC on the surface than the core. In this case, the reading only reflects the MC of the wetter outer surface, regardless of how deep the pins penetrate. To get an accurate core reading with uninsulated pins you can crosscut the board and take a reading of the core on the freshly exposed end grain.

Insulated pins only measure the MC of the wood at the tips of the pins. They come with the external probe accessory that's available with some meters.

Minimum Sample Size

Pinless meters have a minimum sample size that's dictated by the size of the sensor plate. The entire plate must be touching the wood you're testing. So, a meter with a 2 in. x 2 in. sensor pad can't be used on a board that's only 1½-in. wide. This precludes using most pinless meters to scan the edges of 4/4 boards stacked in a pile.

Moisture Content Range

A range of 7 to 20 percent is all you need to check air-dried or kiln-dried wood. You can pay extra for a meter with a range that exceeds 30 percent, but keep in mind that accurate readings higher than 30 percent are impossible because there is just too much water in the wood. People who dry their own wood use the higher readings to get a relative sense of how wet the wood is to start and how fast it's drying. Turners and carvers who work with green wood may benefit from a meter with an extended range.

At the low end of the MC scale, pin meters are accurate down to 7 percent and pinless, down to 5 percent. Readings below these levels are unreliable because there is just too little water in the wood.

Displays

Both types of meters come in one of four types of displays (photo 4, page 79): analog, LED (light emitting diode), digital LED and digital LCD (liquid crystal display). We like the digital LED and digital LCD best. Analog displays are inconvenient.

A "hold" feature on the display is nice to have. Sometimes readings have to be taken in an awkward position or in poor light where it's difficult to read the display. Being able to hold the reading until you can actually see the display can be quite handy.

Some of the more expensive meters give MC readings with a resolution of ¹⁄₁₀ percent. The less expensive meters generally read out larger increments. But, that may be all you need for a go/no-go decision on your wood.

Built-In Species and Temperature Correction

Built-in species correction is a feature you can live without unless you typically need to take readings on a large quantity of wood. A chart can be a hassle, but it's no big deal if you're dealing with just a few boards. Even with built-in correction, you may have to use a chart to find the right setting.

Carrying Cases

Sensor pads and pins need protection when they're being carried around. That's why we liked Delmhorst's tool-box type of carrying case best. It also gives you a place to store charts and manuals that need to travel with your meter. Second best are the ballistic nylon pouches on the Wagner MMC210 and 220. Electrophysics and Moisture Register do not come with carrying cases.

WOOD STABILIZER PREVENTS CRACKS

Q: A recent storm left a large tree limb in our yard. I'd like to slice cross sections for plaques and trivets. How do I keep the slices from splitting as they dry?

A: Pentacryl wood preservative is an excellent product made for this very purpose. A slice of wood will always split because, as it dries, the cells collapse and wither just like a dry sponge. This stress from contraction literally pulls the disk apart, usually resulting in a single, nasty split that runs from the bark edge toward the pith. Pentacryl reinforces the cells so they retain their shape as they dry. As a result, very little stress builds up in the wood and cracks rarely occur. Pentacryl is nontoxic and is compatible with any kind of finish.

Here are a few tips about making plaques from Dale Knobloch, the owner of Preservation Solutions, which makes Pentacryl.

- To keep the bark edge on a slab, cut the wood during the winter.
- Wood that has been outside, especially in winter, should be brought to room temperature before you apply Pentacryl.
- Don't overtreat—plan to soak your wood no more than five minutes for every inch of its thickness.
- After treatment, the wood must be allowed to dry evenly. Make sure it is exposed to air on all sides.
- Don't hurry the drying by adding heat or air movement.

ART DIRECTION: RICK DUPRE • PHOTOGRAPHY: RAMON MORENO

Getting the Most from your Wood-Buying Bucks | 81

by DAVE MUNKITTRICK

Dry Your Own Wood

OUR SIMPLE KILN BEATS THE HIGH COST OF WOOD

It's been said that in life there are only two sure things: death and taxes. For us woodworkers there's a third; the cost of wood keeps going up! There's not a lot we can do about death and taxes, but there is an antidote to the high cost of lumber. Build this dehumidification kiln for about $600 and you can save 50 to 80 percent on the cost of store-bought lumber. The kiln will pay for itself with the first two or three loads of hardwood you dry!

We'll start by showing how the kiln works and then give you detailed instruction on how to build it. After the kiln is built, we'll show you how to prepare green wood for drying and how to operate the kiln to maintain a safe drying rate that guarantees great results.

The AW Kiln:
A Simple, Practical Design

There are small commercial dehumidification kiln kits available, but they cost $2,300 and up and you still have to build the kiln box yourself. Our design is centered around a standard household dehumidifier (around $180), with controls made from stock electrical components. A household dehumidifier won't last as long as a heavier-duty commercial unit, but we've run about 1,000 bd. ft. through our prototype kiln over the past year and its Sears dehumidifier is still going strong.

The kiln itself is basically a big plywood box that holds the dehumidifier, lights and a fan. The light bulbs supply auxiliary heat to the kiln, and are needed mostly at the beginning of the drying cycle, when the dehumidifier is not running all the time. We used an attic ventilator fan to circulate the air because it's designed to operate in warm conditions.

The humidistat and thermostat make it easy to set and control the drying environment inside your kiln. However, if you plan on using your kiln to only dry air-dried lumber or construction-grade pine, you can do without the humidistat and thermostat. The kiln can be run full tilt once the wood has been dried below 20-percent moisture content.

You can buy green lumber from many sawmills at a fraction of the price of kiln-dried lumber from a dealer. With the AW kiln, you can dry green lumber yourself, gently, and to perfect moisture levels. **Note:** Guard removed for clarity.

Schmitt Timber, Spring Valley, WI

For safety reasons, we've added a high-temperature limit switch to the kiln (see "Kiln Controls" page 84).

Because finding space for a kiln may be a problem, we're offering two sizes. The small kiln can handle 100 bd. ft. of 4-ft.-long lumber. This may seem like an odd size, but most furniture can be made using 4-ft. stock. Plus, 4-ft. boards are easy to handle and 4-ft. logs are small enough for you and a buddy to saw into boards on a 14-in. bandsaw.

Note: To size the kiln to handle 8-ft. boards, simply make the box longer and add a light fixture or two. Everything else stays the same.

If you're still worried about where you're going to put the kiln, keep in mind that this kiln is designed to knock-down for storage when not in use.

How the AW Kiln Works

You can see how the AW kiln works or page 84. Generally speaking, it takes about two to six weeks to dry a full load of lumber, depending on the species and thickness.

Having a pin-type moisture meter is essential to drying wood with a kiln. We found it useful to attach wires to a couple boards inside the kiln, so their moisture content could be monitored without opening the kiln. A remote temperature/humidity sensor tells you the conditions inside the kiln.

How to Build the AW Kiln

The woodworking part of this project is easy; all you need is a circular saw, a drill and a weekend. Begin by gathering all the materials listed on page 96 (see Sources, page 204).

The materials for the kiln were chosen for their ability to withstand high humidity, so don't make substitutions. It's important to use exterior-grade plywood (not chipboard), the proper paint and stainless steel fasteners. However, it's okay to use ¾-in. plywood if you can't find ⅝ in.

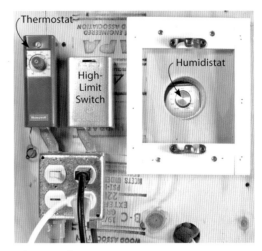

Kiln Controls

The electrical mounting board includes controls for the temperature and humidity, and a high-limit switch, which shuts off power to the kiln should any electrical malfunction result in too high a temperature. The humidistat has to be mounted inside the kiln, so you reach it through a hole covered by a removable access panel.

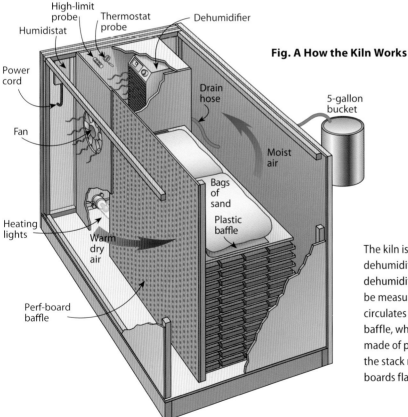

Fig. A How the Kiln Works

The kiln is simply an insulated box, with the dehumidifier at one end. Water from the dehumidifier is collected in a bucket, where it can be measured to tell you the rate of drying. A fan circulates the warm, drier air through a perf-board baffle, which spreads it out evenly. A second baffle, made of plastic film, keeps the air flowing through the stack rather than over it. Weights keep the boards flat as they dry.

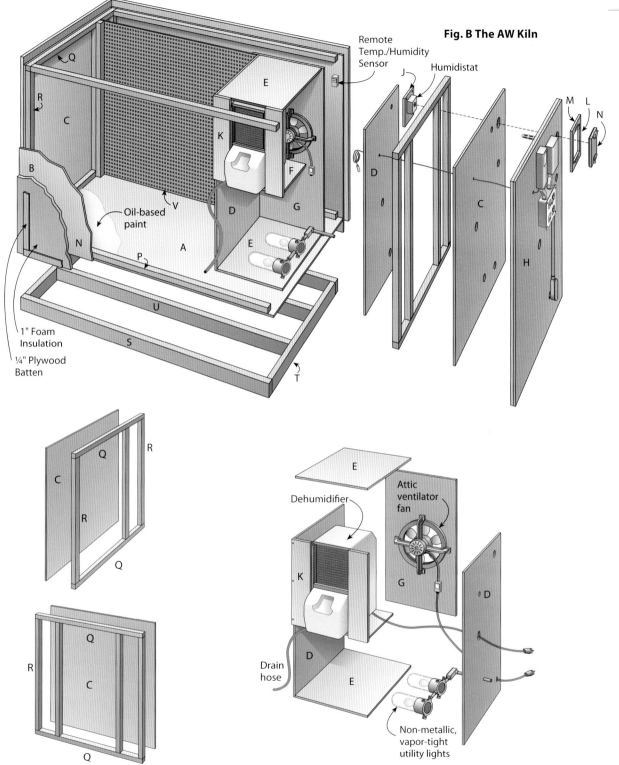

Fig. B The AW Kiln

Remote Temp./Humidity Sensor

Humidistat

Oil-based paint

1" Foam Insulation

¼" Plywood Batten

Fig. C End Panels

Dehumidifier

Attic ventilator fan

Drain hose

Non-metallic, vapor-tight utility lights

Fig. D Dehumidifier Box

Construction

1. Cut all parts according to the Cutting List on page 90. Leave cleats (P and R) a bit long and trim to fit later.

2. Paint all interior surfaces (smooth side of plywood) and cleats with oil-based paint. Be sure to paint the end grain of the cleats.

3. Assemble the 2x4 base (S, T and U) with screws (Photo 1). It's essential that the base be exactly flush with the plywood sides of the kiln to allow the foam insulation to run right down to the floor.

4. Attach the cleats (Q and R) to the end panels (C) (Fig. C).

5. Screw the bottom (A) into the cleats of the assembled end panels (Photo 2).

6. Cut and fit the long cleats (P) and attach them to the bottom panel.

7. Assemble the dehumidifier box (D, E and F) with butt joints and stainless steel screws.

8. Attach the dehumidifier box to the side.

9. Cut a hole in the fan-mounting board (G) using the template included with the fan.

10. Secure a portable power cord in a ½-in. strain-relief-cord connector and attach to the bottom of the fan-control module. (Do not discard this module even though the temperature sensor in it is not used for the kiln.)

11. Attach the fan and the control module to the mounting board. The temperature control that comes attached to the fan should be set on its lowest setting so the fan will always be on.

Build It

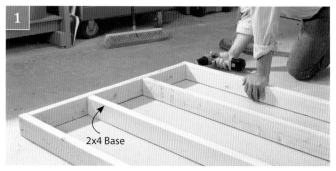

Assemble the base from 2x4s, so it has exactly the same outside dimensions as the plywood box. Set the box on the base and screw them together.

Assemble the box by screwing prepainted pieces of exterior plywood to 2x2 cleats. It's easiest to make the ends first, attach the bottom plywood (as shown), and then fit 2x2 cleats to the edges of the bottom plywood.

The fan and dehumidifier fit in a box at one end of the kiln. Install the back after mounting the fan to the plywood.

Build It *(continued)*

A piece of perf-board screwed along the back of the kiln acts as a baffle to distribute the air evenly through your stack of lumber.

2x2 Cleat

Perf-board baffle

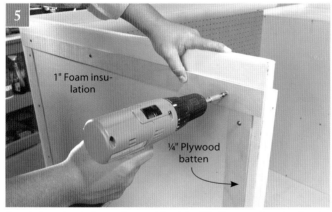

1" Foam insulation

¼" Plywood batten

Attach foam insulation to the outside of the kiln. Use round washer-head screws and thin battens to hold the foam in place.

Mount the electrical boxes and conduit to the end of the kiln before you do any wiring. Keep all the connections loose until you have all the parts mounted. Once you're sure they'll fit, tighten the locknuts with a hammer and screwdriver.

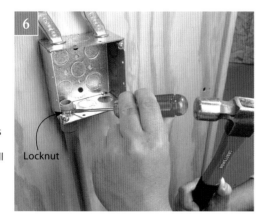

Locknut

12. Attach the fan-mounting board to the back of the dehumidifier box (Photo 3).

13. Attach a 2x2 cleat to one end of the perf-board baffle and attach the baffle to the fan-mounting board and end panel (Photo 4).

14. Attach the back (B).

15. Add foam insulation to the back and sides of the kiln (Photo 5).

16. Attach the electrical mounting board (H) to create a sandwich with the 1-in. insulation board (Fig. B).

17. Build the light-fixture assembly (Fig. E), including the PVC elbow (LB), and drill ⅛-in.-weep holes in the bottom (as mounted) of both the lights and the LB.

18. Run the wires but leave the cover off the conduit LB and let an additional 4 ft. of wire extend out of it. Set this assembly to the side.

19. Drill a hole for the high-temperature-limit sensor and mount it to the electrical mounting board (Fig. F).

20. Set the shut-off limit at 140-degrees F (Fig. E, Detail 2).

21. Install a ½-in.-offset nipple between the left hole in the bottom of the high-temperature-limit switch and the right hole on the top of the 4-in.-square junction box.

22. Attach the junction box to the kiln and install a #10-32 green ground screw.

23. Install and secure the control body of the remote-bulb thermostat switch to the left knock out on top of the 4-in. junction box with a ½-in.-offset nipple.

24. Hand tighten the locknut.

25. Cement a ½-in.-male adapter on one end of a 20-in. section of ½-in.-PVC conduit and a ½-in. LB on the other. Drill a ⅛-in.-weep hole in the bottom of the LB (as mounted).

26. Connect the conduit to the bottom of the 4-in. junction box with a locknut (hand tighten).

27. Use the back entrance in the LB to mark the center of the hole into the dehumidifier compartment.

28. Drill a 1⅛-in. hole about 1-in. deep (to allow for the LB hub to recess) and then continue to drill into the interior of the dehumidifier compartment with a ⅞-in. bit.

29. Remove the 20-in.-PVC section and set it aside for the moment.

30. Cut a 6-in. length of ½-in. PVC and insert it into the light assembly LB (without cement).

31. From the inside of the kiln, insert the ½-in.-PVC stub into the ⅞-in. hole and attach the light assembly to the inside wall of the dehumidifier compartment.

32. Mark the ½-in. PVC flush with the outside wall of the kiln, remove the ½-in. PVC, cut to length. Reinsert the PVC and cement it to the light assembly LB.

33. Insert the male adapter on the 20-in.-PVC section into the 4-in. junction box and cement the LB to the ½-in.-PVC stub that connects to the light assembly LB.

34. Install a ½-in. locknut on the threads of the male adapter and hand tighten.

Build It *(continued)*

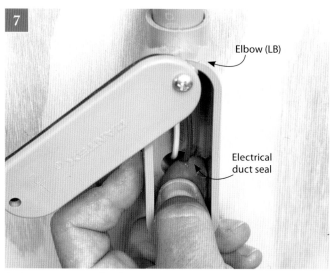

Seal any gaps, especially where wires enter the kiln. The air in the kiln is hot and moist, and wherever it escapes, condensation is likely to occur.

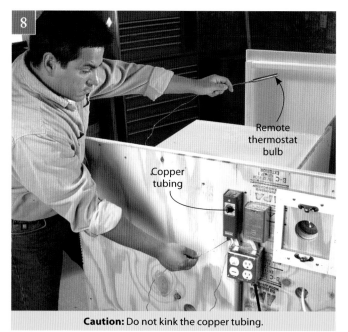

Caution: Do not kink the copper tubing.

Insert the remote thermostat bulb into the kiln, and make a small door on the outside of the kiln that allows access to the controls and the humidistat.

35. Secure the 20-in.-PVC section onto the electrical mounting board with a ½-in.-PVC strap, as shown (Fig. E).

36. Finish tightening all of the locknuts (photo 6, page 87).

37. Thread the 4 ft. of purple and white wire through the LBs and PVC to the 4-in. junction box.

38. Work electrical duct seal into both LBs, being careful not to plug the weep holes (Photo 7).

39. Finish running wires and making connections in the junction box, temperature switch and high-temperature-limit switch.

40. Drill holes for the dehumidifier cord, the humidistat port and cord, the thermostat bulb and the fan cord (Fig. F).

41. Hang the humidistat on the mounting board (J) and hang the assembly inside the kiln (Fig. A).

42. The wireless temperature/humidity sensor can be mounted just below the humidistat.

43. Use scrap plywood to build a frame around the humidistat port. Cut a plywood panel to fit inside the frame and add self-stick weather strip to the backside of the panel. Use window-sash locks to keep the panel shut tight.

44. Uncoil the remote temperature-sensing bulb for the thermostat and carefully thread it through the hole and into the dehumidifier box (Photo 8). Warning:

Don't let the copper coil kink. The coil is a liquid-filled tube, so a kink could cause a leak and ruin your thermostat.

45. At this point, you should plug in all components and give the kiln a test run. Caution: The fan is unguarded, so keep your fingers away!

46. Attach the back (B) and top (A) and add the foam. Leave the 2-in. foam loose on the top, because you may need to prop it up or remove it for temperature control.

47. Use window air-conditioner foam (available at home centers and hardware stores) to plug all the holes where wires come through the electrical panel.

48. Now, set the kiln in place (Photo 9).

Use shims to fill the gaps from an uneven floor. It's important for the kiln base to be well supported. A twist in the base will mean a twist in your wood.

Detail 1: Junction Box Wiring

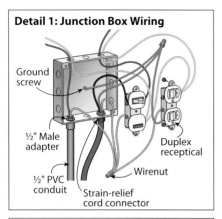

Ground screw

½" Male adapter

½" PVC conduit

Strain-relief cord connector

Wirenut

Duplex receptical

Detail 2: High-Temp.-Limit Switch

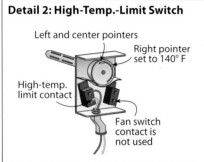

Left and center pointers

Right pointer set to 140° F

High-temp. limit contact

Fan switch contact is not used

Fig. E: Wiring

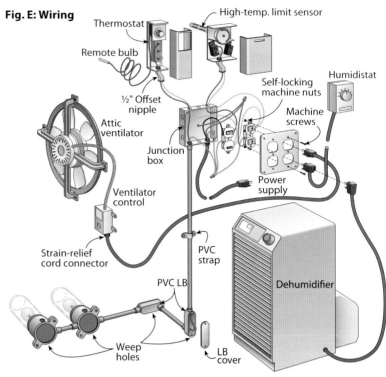

High-temp. limit sensor

Thermostat

Remote bulb

½" Offset nipple

Attic ventilator

Junction box

Self-locking machine nuts

Humidistat

Machine screws

Power supply

Strain-relief cord connector

Ventilator control

PVC strap

PVC LB

Weep holes

LB cover

Dehumidifier

Fig. F: Electrical Mounting Board

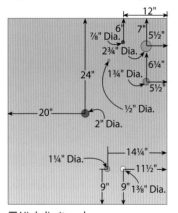

12"
6"
7"
5½"
⅞" Dia.
2¾" Dia.
6¼"
24"
1¾" Dia.
5½"
20"
½" Dia.
2" Dia.
1¼" Dia.
14¼"
11½"
9" 9" 1⅜" Dia.

■ High-limit probe
◻ Conduit elbow (LB)
■ Dehumidifier cord
◻ Humidistat port
■ Humidistat cord
◻ Remote thermostat bulb
◻ Fan cord

Note: Hole locations are given as guidelines. Only the high-limit sensor needs to be placed exactly.

Cutting List
Overall Dimensions: 47"H x 80"W x 43¾"D

Part	Name	Qty.	Dimensions	Material
A	Top and bottom	2	40" x 78"	⅝" BC Fir Ply
B	Front and back	2	41¼" x 78"	
C	Ends	2	40" x 40"	
D	Dehumid. box sides	2	24" x 40"	
E	Dehumid. box top & bottom	2	21½" x 24"	
F	Dehumid. shelf	1	21½" x 14"	
G	Fan mounting board	1	24" x 40"	
H	Electrical mounting board	1	41¼" x 47"	
J	Humidistat mounting board	1	6" x 8"	
K	Dehumidifier flange	2	5¼" x 22½"	
L	Humidistat access frame	2	1" x 10"	
M	Humidistat access frame	2	2" x 6"	
N	Humidistat access cover	1	6" x 6"	
P	Cleats	4	74" (rough)	2x2 Stock
Q	Cleats	5	40"	
R	Cleats	7	39" (rough)	
S	Base	2	78"	Floor Base 2x4 Stock
T	Base	2	38¼"	
U	Base	2	75"	
V	Baffle	1	40" x 50¾"	¼-in. Perf-Board

Cut foam and ¼" battens to fit kiln.

Load It

Seal the ends of each board with 2 to 3 coats of commercial end-sealer. It should be thick enough to dig your fingernail into. The sealer should extend at least ½ in. up the surface of the board. The boards must be trimmed to approximately the same size, and all—absolutely all—end-checks removed.

Measure the dimensions of each board (LxWxThickness). Multiply those dimensions to give the exact volume of each board, and add these all together to get the total volume of wood in the kiln. Divide by 144 to convert this to bd. ft. If you know the exact volume of wood in the kiln, you'll be able to determine how much water can safely be extracted in a day.

Hammer a pair of ¾-in. brads into boards that will be on the bottom, middle and top of the pile. The brads should go halfway into the boards, in the middle of the face, and parallel to the grain. Attach wire leads to the brads, and you can measure the moisture content of the boards from outside the kiln.

Drying Your Wood

Once your kiln is built, you're ready to go get some green wood! Even if you live in the desert Southwest, a little poking around will yield an abundant supply of fresh green wood. Here are a few possibilities:

- Cut your own. With a shop-made sled to hold the log, you can cut lumber with a standard 14-in. bandsaw.
- Check the Yellow Pages under "Sawmills." You may find some local mills that sell green wood or someone with a portable mill who can come to you and the tree.
- Call local tree services or your city's forestry service and find out what they're doing with their felled trees.

You can also use your kiln to dry home center softwood to a useable moisture level in a matter of days. You don't even need to use the kiln controls; just let it go full blast.

Winter is Best

Winter is the best time to harvest green wood. Lower temperatures reduce moisture loss from the log end, greatly reducing the risk of end-checking. In addition, the mold spores that can cause discoloration of light species, like maple and pine, are dormant. It's still a good idea to seal the ends of valuable logs and boards even if they're going to be sitting out in the cold for a while.

In warm weather, freshly cut boards must be trimmed, end-sealed and loaded into the kiln or stacked for air-drying within hours. Make sure you budget enough time to complete the job!

Trim and Seal the Boards

It's essential to trim the ends of each board, to eliminate any checks that may have formed since the boards were first cut from the log. Don't be tempted to leave even a tiny check in a board; it will only get worse as the wood dries. It's okay to cut a board a little short in order to completely remove an end check. When you're trimming the ends, try to make boards of uniform length (4-ft. for our basic kiln).

The freshly cut ends are then sealed with end sealer (photo 1, page 91). We like Dura-Seal, an oil-based end sealer, or Anchor Seal, a water-based sealer. Both products are designed to adhere to wet wood, even in below-freezing temperatures. You may be tempted to use up old paint, but don't—an imperfect seal will result. End coating is essential because boards lose moisture very rapidly out of the end grain. This results in the ends of the boards drying much faster than the center, a sure recipe for a pile of expensive firewood.

Loading the Kiln

Once the boards have been cut and sealed, you're ready to stack the wood in the kiln.

Prepare a base for your stack by placing 4x4s or doubled 2x4s every 16 in.

Next, make stickers for your pile. Stickers are small pieces of dry wood that run perpendicular to the boards and separate each layer of wood in the stack. Cut lumberyard pine into ¾ x ¾-in. stickers for the middle of the stack. Use 1x2s at the ends of the boards. The wider stickers accommodate variations in board length.

Load It *(continued)*

Build the pile. Use full-length boards on the outer edges, stagger the short boards, and use offcuts to fill any voids over a sticker. Keep the stickers aligned vertically, with doubled 2x4s at the bottom of the pile below the stickers.

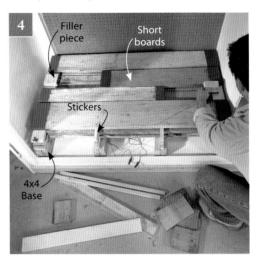

Labels: Filler piece; Short boards; Stickers; 4x4 Base

Labels: Plastic baffle; Plywood roof

5 Drop the plastic baffle over the pile. The plastic baffle keeps all the air moving through the pile rather than over the top of it. The plastic baffle is secured to the top of the perf-board baffle with screws and a strip of 2-in.-wide, ¼-in. plywood. Place a piece of scrap plywood on the top of the pile, then weight the top as heavily as possible.

Load It *(continued)*

6 All loaded and ready to go! We weighted the top of our pile with sandbags wrapped in black plastic garbage bags.

Measure each board that gets loaded into the kiln and write it down (photo 2, page 91). In order to effectively use the safe drying rate (SDR) table on page 97 you'll need to know exactly how many bd. ft. of lumber is in the kiln.

As you stack the boards, keep all the edges in the same plane. Try for a perfect shoe-box shape. This helps create even airflow throughout the stack. Leave a 6-in. gap between the front of the pile and the front of the kiln for a cold-air return.

Set a pair of ¾-in. brads into the middle of the front board in the first layer of wood (photo 3, page 91). Wires attached to the brads act as remote sensors for monitoring the wood as it dries, without

Give it a test before you screw on the front.
- Turn up the thermostat until the lights go on. Use fresh bulbs for each load.
- Turn down the humidistat until the dehumidifier goes on.
- Plug in the fan and make sure air is flowing through the stack.
- Check the remote temperature/humidity sensor; it should register a temperature rise.

Attach the front, fishing the remote probe wires through holes in the front. Screw on the insulation and you're ready to start drying.

having to open up the kiln. As you build the stack, add sensors to a board in the middle and top layer.

As you build the stack, keep all the stickers in perfect vertical alignment. Always use full-length boards on the outside of the stack. Short boards are placed in the middle. Stagger the short ends so the voids aren't all on one end of the pile (photo 4, page 92).

Once you've loaded all the wood, lay stickers across the top and cover the pile with a plywood lid. Pull a plastic sheet or baffle down from the top of the perf-board baffle and lay it over the plywood (photo 5, page 92). Add weight to the top of the pile. We used bags of sand wrapped in heavy-duty garbage bags. The weight locks the boards in place and minimizes warping and twisting (photo 6, page 93).

Before you seal up the kiln, give it a test (photo 7, page 93). If everything's working, attach the front (photo 8, page 93) and you're ready to start drying your wood!

Operating the Kiln

Take initial readings from all three remote sensors and write them down. Refer to the SDR chart on page 97 for initial temperature and humidity settings. The initial settings are derived from long-established dry kiln schedules.

After the first 8 to 12 hours of operation, measure the water in the collection bucket (photo 2, right) and compare your findings with the SDR chart on page 97. Adjust the humidistat up or down to keep the drying rate just below the SDR for that species. When the amount of water collected in a

Run It

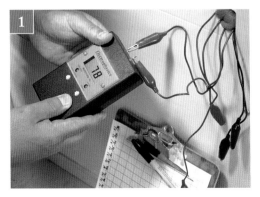

Take an initial moisture content (MC) reading with a pin-type moisture meter. Record the results on a chart, along with the date and time.

Measure the water that comes out of the dehumidifier after 8 to 12 hours. Figure out the water loss per bd. ft. per hour and compare it with the safe drying rate (SDR) given on page 97. Adjust the humidistat to stay at or below the SDR. Continue measuring the water and adjusting the humidistat until the wood is below 20-percent MC.

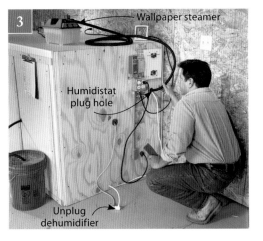

Wallpaper steamer

Humidistat plug hole

Unplug dehumidifier

After the wood is dry, condition it to remove drying stresses. Unplug the dehumidifier, set the thermostat to 125 degrees F and use a rented wallpaper steamer to raise the relative humidity in the kiln to 85 to 90 percent.

Run It *(continued)*

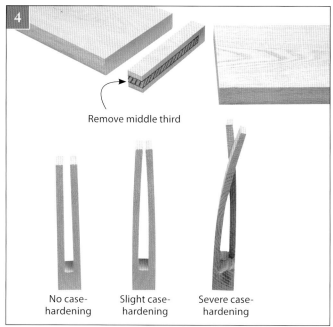

Remove middle third

No case-hardening

Slight case-hardening

Severe case-hardening

Test for casehardening by cutting a "tuning fork" from the center of one board. Casehardening is a form of drying stress that can result in cupping or warping when the boards are cut. If your boards are severely casehardened, they'll need more conditioning and more time to settle.

Oops!

Butternut and oak sure look alike when they're in the rough! We accidentally loaded a few oak boards in with our butternut load. Butternut is a low-density wood and can be dried quickly, so the red oak suffered the consequences of being dried too fast. Talk about a casehardening problem. Plus, there were a number of surface checks in the oak. Well, lesson learned— don't mix species in the kiln unless they share similar safe drying rates.

butternut   Red oak

day begins to fall off, you can safely lower the humidistat setting about 5 percent. Keep measuring and lowering the humidity based on the amount of water collected. Keep an eye on the temperature. It will gradually rise as the dehumidifier runs more frequently. If the temperature gets up over 120 degrees F, prop up a corner of the insulation to let it escape.

Once the MC drops below 20 percent, the humidistat will probably be set as low as it can go and the dehumidifier will be running constantly. There's nothing more to do except measure the water extracted and take moisture content (MC) readings. Once the MC reaches the lower teens, little or no water will be coming out of the kiln. This doesn't mean the drying has stopped. The little water that's left in the wood is hard to extract, especially at the relatively low temperatures at which this kiln operates. Rely on your moisture meter to tell you when the wood is sufficiently dry.

A Typical Example

Say you have 100 bd. ft. of 4/4 hard maple in the kiln. Check the chart on page 97 for the initial temperature and humidity settings (190-degrees F and 81 percent). Let the kiln run for about 12 hours, then measure the water collected in the bucket.

Next, determine the amount of water you can safely extract from your wood per hour by consulting the SDR chart. The SDR for soft maple is .0074 pints per hour per bd. ft. Because you have 100 bd ft. in the kiln, your load can safely produce .74 pints of water an hour. If you measure the extracted water after the first 12 hours of operation, you would multiply .74 by 12 to get 8.88 pints of water (call it 8¾ pints) that can safely be removed from your load of hard maple in a 12-hour period. If you measured 8 pints from the kiln, you're safe; don't touch that dial! If you're a bit over, say 10 pints in a 12-hour period, turn the humidistat up 5 percent.

Remember, never exceed the safe drying rate. The SDR is based on 24-hour periods. If you accidentally exceed the rate for a short time, don't fret, but don't take that as an invitation to push the kiln. The time you save is not worth the risk ruining your load of wood. You can't make up for going over the rate one day by going under the rate the next because the damage has already occurred.

Take measurements frequently at first, until the kiln settles in. Measure the water at least once a day and lower the humidistat to maintain the SDR until the moisture content readings drop below 20 percent. Remember, most drying defects occur as the wood goes from the dead green state to about 30-percent moisture content.

Continue monitoring the kiln every few days until you achieve moisture meter readings of 7 to 8 percent. At that point your wood is dry. But don't be overly anxious to see your wood just yet. Unplug the kiln and let it cool down for a few days or you run the risk of the boards warping. Once cool, the wood should be "conditioned" to relieve some of the casehardening that occurs as wood dries (see Conditioning, page 97).

Materials
Kiln Box

Qty.	Name
7	⅝-in. 4x8 BC fir plywood
1	¼-in. 4x8 perf-board
1	¼-in. ply (for battens)
5	8-ft. 2x4s
8	8-ft. 2x2s
1	2-in. 4x8 polystyrene
3	1-in. 4x8 polystyrene
1	Garden hose
1	Self-stick ½-in. foam weatherstrip
1	Window AC foam
2	150-watt light bulbs
2	Barn lights
3	Boxes of stainless steel screws: 100 8 x 1½-in,
1	Box of 100 8 x 1½-in. round washer head screws
End grain sealer	

Electrical

Qty.	Name
1	4-in. sq. x 2⅛-in. deep metal junction box with ½-in. knock-outs
1	4-in. sq. ½-in. raised cover that can hold 2 standard duplex receptacles
1	15-amp, 125-volt duplex outlet
1	combination single-pole switch and pilot light (pilot light requires a neutral for the light to work while the switch is on)
2	14/3 portable cord (S, SJ or SJT typ.)
2	½-in. portable cord clamp that fits the 14/3 cord
2	½-in. offset nipples
4	½-in. locknuts
5 ft.	½-in. rigid non-metallic conduit (schedule 40 or 80 PVC)
1	½-in. two-pole PVC strap
1	½-in. PVC male adapter
2	½-in. PVC service elbow (LB)
1	#10-32 ground screw
8	Wirenuts
1	Remote bulb thermostat
1	Fan/high-temp.-limit switch
1	Humidistat
1	Attic exhaust fan with control and switch
1	Small dehumidifier
1	Wireless thermometer/ hygrometer
1	Pack of PK-10 jumper leads
1 lb. plug of electrical duct seal	
14 ga. THHN solid wire	

Safe Drying Rates

(in pints per hour per bd. ft.)
for common species, 4/4 stock

Species	Initial Temp. = 90-degrees F	
	4/4 SDR*	Initial Relative Humidity†
Ash, Black	.0068	81%
Ash, White or Green	.0060	81%
Aspen, Cottonwood, Poplar	.0114	83%
Atlantic White Cedar	.0074	84%
Basswood	.0083	55%
Beech	.0061	89%
Birch, White	.0052	82%
Birch, Yellow	.0060	81%
Cherry, Black	.0071	81%
Elm, Rock	.0043	85%
Elm, White, American	.0100	80%
Fir, Balsam	.0143	77%
Hemlock, Eastern	.0165	84%
Hickory	.0078	86%
Larch, Eastern	.0208	82%
Maple, Hard	.0061	81%
Maple, Soft	.0074	81%
Oak, Red Southern	.0023	90%
Oak, Red Upland	.0046	87%
Oak, White	.0031	87%
Pine, Eastern White	.0088	76%
Pine, Red (Norway)	.0133	84%
Spruce, Black	.0165	83%
Spruce, Red	.0160	83%
Spruce, White	.0150	83%
Sweetgum (red gum)	.0053	81%
Tupelo (black gum)	.0110	77%
Walnut	.0088	80%

* for 6/4 stock, multiply SDR by .6
   for 8/4 stock, multiply by .4

† add 5 percent to relative humidity
   for 8/4 stock

Conditioning

No matter how wood is dried, it will have some degree of casehardening. Casehardening is a drying stress created in the early stages of drying. As the outer surface dries, it tries to shrink, but the still-wet inner core prevents it. This sets up stress. Casehardened wood will pinch the saw when ripped and cup when resawn, because the wood moves when the stress is relieved.

Conditioning uses steam to quickly add moisture to the outer surface of the boards. Now the outer surface tries to swell but the dry core again prevents it. The net effect is that the stress of conditioning counteracts the stress of casehardening. Seems crazy doesn't it?

To condition your boards, rent or buy a wallpaper steamer and run the hose into the kiln (photo 3, page 94). With the fan and lights on, run the steamer until the humidity climbs into the upper 80s and the temperature reaches about 125 degrees F. After one hour you can turn off the steamer and the lights, if you're conditioning a low-density wood like basswood. For higher density woods like oak or maple, or for thicker stock, condition the wood a few hours longer before shutting down the heat and steam. Keep the fan running and let the kiln cool down for three days.

Open the kiln and remove a sample board to check for casehardening. Cut a tuning-fork shape out of the middle of a board (photo 4, page 95). If the tines don't touch, there is minimal casehardening, so you can safely unload the wood and stack it with stickers in your shop or storage area. If they do touch, seal the kiln back up and condition the load again.

by DAVE MUNKITTRICK

Solar Kiln

DRY YOUR OWN WOOD FAST AND HASSLE-FREE

Wood is expensive. And extra-wide or figured wood is practically beyond reach. Over the 25-plus years I've been a professional woodworker, wood seems to have taken a cue from oil: The price keeps going up. There are ways to use less oil, but when a project requires 100 bd. ft. of walnut, you gotta buy 100 bd. ft. of walnut. That's why I was so thrilled to discover a simple solar kiln developed by Dr. Eugene Wengert, an extension forest products specialist at the University of Wisconsin–Madison.

Wood is relatively inexpensive before it's dry. I have managed to obtain green wood at a lumberyard at a fraction of the price of dry wood. Granted, there is a fair amount of sweat equity involved in stacking and transporting larger amounts of wood, but the savings are well worth the effort.

A solar kiln is the simplest and safest way to dry green wood quickly. Because the wood is protected from the elements, this solar kiln offers more control with much less chance of defects than air-drying provides. Unlike air-drying, it'll dry wood to the moisture level needed for interior use. And unlike other kilns, it is designed so that it's nearly impossible to dry 4/4 wood too fast. It's as close as you can get to a "set it and forget it" system. After the kiln is loaded, all that's required is some minimal vent adjusting while the wood dries. No sweating over daily drying rates and continual monitoring of the drying process.

I talked with a number of solar-kiln owners for this article. I discovered they all share one problem: where to store all their wonderful solar-dried wood.

Set It and Forget It

The beauty of this solar kiln design is that it's almost impossible to dry 4/4 wood too quickly. Even so, most hardwoods can be dried in six weeks during the peak summer months. Our load of basswood took only four weeks. A conventional kiln dries the wood continuously and has to be monitored closely to prevent

Dave's stylish golf bag

With this kiln, you really can "set it and forget it." While your wood dries, you can get back to your shop or other interests.

Dry Anything

With care, a solar kiln can dry wood pieces that are just about any shape or size. You can often dry mixed species and thicknesses in the same load. A solar kiln makes it easy.

Great Wood at an Unbelievable Price

Buying wood green and drying it yourself saves a lot of money. The big pile of green wood in front cost the same as the tiny pile of kiln-dried wood behind me.

exceeding the safe drying rate for that species (see "Safe Drying Rates," page 105). A solar kiln is cyclical (Fig. A). During the day, the kiln heats up and the fan comes on to circulate hot air through the stack. Moisture is drawn from the wood into the air and is vented outside through the vents or leaks out naturally through the kiln's joints and seams. At night, the cooling cycle begins. The temperature drops, the fan shuts down and the moist air condenses. The surface of the wood gets wet and cool, relieving any drying stresses that built up during the day. It's like having an automatic conditioning cycle built in.

For most 4/4 stock, it's OK to start with the vents open an inch or two (photo 8, page 105). This helps remove the moist air quickly. At the same time, however, you're also letting out heat, so there is a trade-off. After the majority of the moisture is out of the wood, which usually takes a week or two, go ahead and shut the vents to maximize the temperature. Moisture can still escape the kiln because it's not airtight.

For figured, thick, prized, or check-prone wood, it's best to start the drying process with the vents closed. This keeps the humidity in the kiln from dropping too quickly and slows the drying process. This is especially necessary with stock thicker than 4/4. (For fast-drying or white woods, leave the vents wide open until the wood reaches 20 percent moisture content.) After a few weeks with the vents closed, most of the moisture will be out of the wood. Open the vents a few inches to help expel the remaining moisture. Shut the vents for the

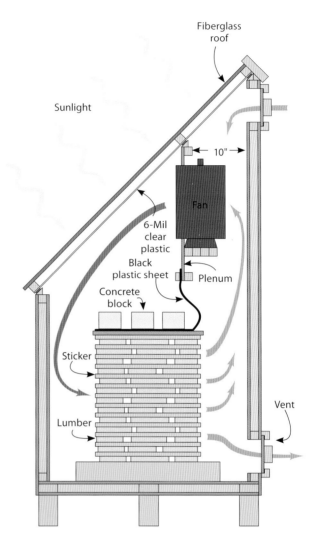

Fig. A: How It Works

Solar energy enters the kiln through the fiberglass roof. The sun's radiant energy hits the dark interior and heats the kiln. A timer is set to run the fan from about one hour after sunrise to one hour after sunset. As the kiln heats up during the day, the fan circulates warm air through the lumber stack. A plastic sheet forms a baffle that forces air only through the stack. The moving air picks up moisture from the wet wood and is vented out the back. **NOTE:** Opening the vents allows you to release moist air more rapidly. The kiln is not airtight, so moisture-laden air can escape even with the vents closed. At night, the fan shuts down, the kiln cools and the moisture from the air condenses, wetting the boards. This conditions the wood and eases any drying stresses built up during the day. This process practically guarantees good results without daily monitoring. I dried 4/4 red oak in six weeks with virtually no checking.

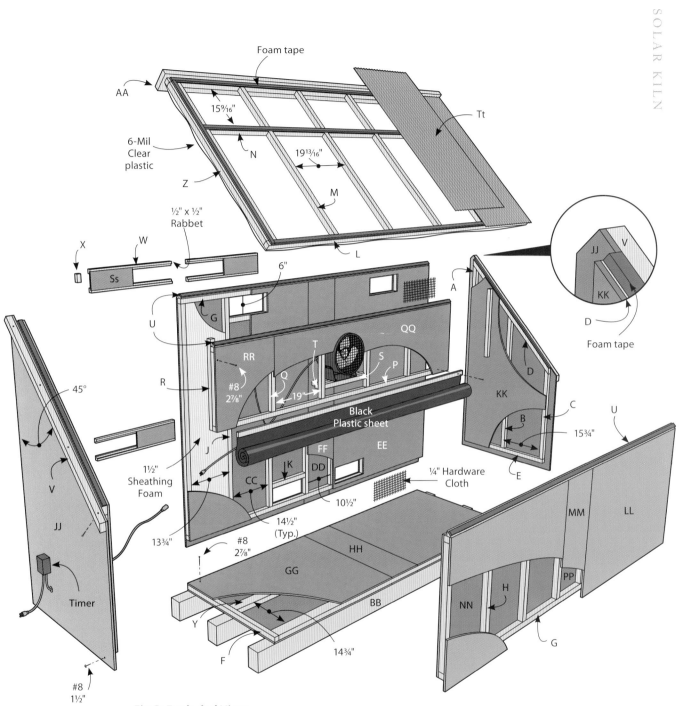

Foam tape

AA

15⁹⁄₁₆"

6-Mil Clear plastic

N

19¹³⁄₁₆"

Z

M

Tt

½" x ½" Rabbet

X

W

Ss

6"

L

A

JJ   V

KK

D

Foam tape

U

G

RR

T

QQ

S

P

45°

R

#8 2⁷⁄₈"

Q

19"

D

KK

C

1½" Sheathing Foam

J

Black Plastic sheet

B

15¾"

U

V

K

FF

EE

E

JJ

CC

DD

¼" Hardware Cloth

MM

LL

13¾"

14½" (Typ.)

10½"

Timer

#8 2⁷⁄₈"

HH

PP

Y

GG

BB

NN

H

F

14¾"

G

#8 1½"

Fig.B: Exploded View

SOLAR KILN

last week or so. You may find it's easiest to simply leave the vents closed all the time for thick or hard-to-dry wood.

Drying thicker wood does require some monitoring of the drying rate. For safe drying rates, see "Safe Drying Rates" (page 105). To slow the drying process for thick wood or when the kiln is less than full, you can block off parts of the roof with an opaque covering or tarp. You can learn all there is to know about solar kilns and wood drying at *www.woodweb.com*. Click on The Wood Doctor.

Build the Kiln

Building the kiln is straightforward. All the materials are readily available at home centers or lumberyards. The total cost, including a fan and timer, should run about $850. Be sure to use corrosion-resistant fasteners throughout the kiln.

The kiln is made up of six panels (Fig. B, page 101)—floor, roof, front, back and sides—that can be built in the comfort of your shop (Photo 1). Insulation in the walls and floor helps the kiln retain heat, which helps speed the drying process. All of the interior surfaces are coated with a flat black oil-based paint. The oil base prevents moisture from penetrating into the wood, and the flat black color absorbs heat from the solar energy.

The solar-panel roof is made with translucent corrugated-fiberglass roofing material. It offers the best combination of low cost and durability. The corrugated roof must be sealed against the roof frame at the

top and bottom edges. Corrugated roofing manufacturers offer various solutions to this problem, such as wood strips cut to match the undulating roofline or strips of foam that conform to the corrugations. To increase the insulating value of the roof, I also stapled clear 6-mil-thick plastic sheeting on the underside of the roof frame. This added layer greatly improves the kiln's performance.

Project Requirements at a Glance

Materials
- 28 2x2 x 8' treated
- 10 2x4 x 10' treated
- One 2x6 x 10' treated
- Three 4x6 x 10' treated
- Seven 1½" x 4' x 8' sheathing foam
- 14½" x 48" x 96" treated plywood
- One 12" ventilation fan
- One multiple-outlet timer
- Five 25½" x 120" corrugated fiberglass panels

Hardware
- Eight ⁷⁄₁₆" x 1¼" x 10' black foam tape
- No. 8 x 2⅞" corrosion-resistant screws
- No. 8 x 1½" corrosion-resistant screws
- Sealing washers
- One fan timer
- One 1,000-cfm fan
- 1-gal. flat black oil-based paint

Tools
- Tablesaw and/or circular saw
- Miter saw
- Drill
- Framing square
- 4-ft. level
- Cost $850

Assemble the Kiln

It's important to locate the kiln with a south-facing exposure that's free of shadows. I set down treated landscape timbers to hold the kiln up off the ground (Photo 2). The timbers provide a level platform for the kiln to rest on. I started by securing the floor to the timbers, then added the back and sides (Photo 3). After attaching the fan plenum (Fig. B, page 101) to cleats mounted on the side panels, I drilled a hole for the fan cord. Finally, the kiln was ready for loading. All I needed was some green wood to dry.

I built the kiln's panels in my shop using deck screws. Foam insulation board helps hold the heat in when the sun is down. Treated wood and plywood resist decay in the high moisture environment of a kiln.

To prepare a base for the kiln, I leveled treated landscape timbers on a bed of river rock in my backyard. A sheet of plastic under the river rock discourages weed growth.

The panels go together easily. I painted the kiln's interior surfaces black to protect the wooden walls against moisture penetration and to help absorb more heat from the sun.

Plenum bottom

Stickers

Timbers

I started the stack with timbers to keep the drying wood up off the wet floor. I stacked the green wood to within about 6 in. of the bottom of the fan plenum. Stickers create a gap between each layer so hot air can be driven through the stack by the fan.

Load the Kiln

Loading the kiln is a breeze with the roof and front panel removed (photo 4, page 103). If you're drying check-prone wood, such as oak, use an end sealer (see Sources, page 204) on the wood before it's stacked. Note: Be sure to stack the wood to leave at least a 6-in. airspace in front and back and under the fan plenum.

I added a couple of remote sensors in the middle of the stack so I could tell when the wood was dry without having to open the kiln (Photo 5). I used a commercial kit (see Sources). You can substitute two nails for the sensors; set them about an inch apart and driven to one-quarter depth of a board. Attach a wire to each nail with alligator clips and run them out a hole in the side of the kiln. To take a reading, simply clip the wires onto the prongs on your moisture meter.

When you're done stacking your green wood, attach a plastic sheet to the bottom of the fan plenum and drape it over the stack (Fig. B). The plastic directs the air so it circulates through the stack. Weight the stack down with cement blocks (Photo 6).

Run an extension cord from the outdoor timer to the fan through a hole drilled in a side panel (Fig. B, page 101). Attach the front panel and the roof (Photo 7) and set the vents (Photo 8). Your green wood is on its way to being kiln-dried.

Cutting List

Overall Dimensions: 109"W x 78¾"T x 41"D

Part	Name	Qty.	Dimensions	Material
A	Side stud	2	68⅜" *	2x2 treated
B	Side stud	2	51⅛"	
C	Side stud	2	33⅞"	
D	Side top plate	2	50¹⁵⁄₁₆" **	
E	Side bottom plate	2	36"	
F	Floor plate	2	40"	
G	Front and back wall plate	4	108"	
H	Front wall stud	8	30½"	
J	Back wall stud	8	69"	
K	Back wall blocking	4	14½"	
L	Roof plate	2	112"	
M	Roof rafter	4	53½"	
N	Roof blocking	5	19¹³⁄₁₆"	
P	Plenum plate	2	104"	
Q	Plenum stud	6	21"	
R	Plenum cleat	2	25¹⁵⁄₁₆"	
S	Fan shelf	3	19"	
T	Fan shelf mount	1	22" ***	
U	Wall cap	4	1¼" x 1¼" x 108"	
V	Roof-attachment cleat	2	57¹¹⁄₁₆"	
W	Door track	8	35"	
X	Door handle	4	3"	
Y	Floor stud	3	105"	2x4 treated
Z	Roof end rafter	2	53½"	
AA	Roof rear lip	1	114"	2x6 treated
BB	Platform	3	120"	4x6 treated
CC	Back (exterior)	2	48" x 74½"	½" treated plywood
DD	Back strip (exterior)	1	12" x 74½"	
EE	Back (interior)	2	48" x 72"	
FF	Back strip (interior)	1	12" x 72"	
GG	Floor	4	48" x 40"	
HH	Floor strip	2	40" x 12"	
JJ	Side (exterior)	2	41" x 75¾"	
KK	Side (interior)	2	36" x 72"	
LL	Front (exterior)	2	48" x 36"	
MM	Front strip (exterior)	1	36" x 12"	
NN	Front (interior)	2	48" x 33½"	
PP	Front strip (interior)	1	12" x 33½"	
QQ	Fan plenum	1	24" x 82¾"	
RR	Fan plenum strip	1	24" x 21¼"	
SS	Door	4	6¾" x 17½"	
TT	Roof panel	5	25½" x 57"	

* Measure to long point of 45-degree cut on the end.

** Measure from long point on one 45-degree end to short point on other 45-degree end.

*** Rip 2x2 stock at 45 degrees.

Safe Drying Rates above 30% Moisture Content (MC)

Species	Maximum Rate of MC Loss Per Day
Beech	4.5%
Birch	6.1%
Hard Maple	6.5%
Soft Maple	13.8%
Red Oak	3.8%
White Oak	2.5%
Walnut	8.2%

The maximum "safe rate" for 2-in. hardwood lumber can be obtained by dividing the 1-in. safe rate by 2.5. Thus, the 2-in. safe rate for beech is 1.8 percent moisture content (MC) loss per day ($4.5 \div 2.5 = 1.8$).

Excerpted from "Processing Trees to Lumber—for the Hobbyist and Small Business" by Eugene M. Wengert and Dan A. Meyer, www.woodweb.com. Click on The Wood Doctor, Kiln Operation, Processing Trees to Lumber.

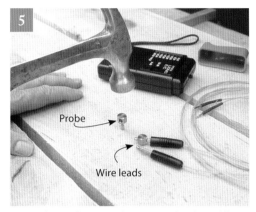

Two probes are hammered into a board in the middle of the stack. Wire leads are run out of the kiln, where a moisture meter can take readings. Sensors allow you to monitor the wood without having to open the kiln.

I topped the stack with cement blocks painted black for heat absorption. The weight from the blocks reduces warping in the drying wood. A plastic sheet attached to the plenum and draped over the top of the stack forces air through the stack.

With the help of a friend, I set the roof on the kiln. The removable roof hooks over the peak and is secured with screws through a cleat on the side.

Vents allow moisture to escape during drying. They are closed toward the end of the drying process to help maximize heat and get the wood down to the target 8 percent MC.

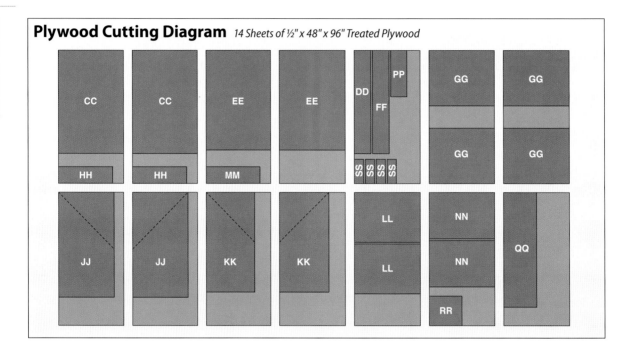

Plywood Cutting Diagram *14 Sheets of ½" x 48" x 96" Treated Plywood*

Kiln Design

I downsized Dr. Wengert's kiln design to dry about 300 bd. ft. of 4/4 wood at a time. I changed the construction a bit so it could be disassembled and stored when not in use. The smaller size allows me to remove the roof and front panel for easy loading. If you wish to alter the size of your kiln, there is an important ratio to remember: For every 10 bd. ft. of capacity, you need 1 sq. ft. of solar-panel or roof area. Too much solar-panel area and you'll run the risk of drying the wood too fast; not enough and you'll never get the wood to dry below 15 percent moisture content (MC). Since my kiln is designed to hold about 300 bd. ft., that dictates a roof area of about 30 sq. ft.

I installed a single fan rated at 1,000 cubic feet per minute (cfm) to circulate air through the stack of wood. A larger kiln will require two such fans for optimum airflow. Shoot for approximately 150 feet per minute (fpm) air velocity through the stack. To calculate the size of fan needed (in cfm), multiply the number of sticker layers by the length in feet of the wood stack times the thickness in feet of the stickers (¾ in. equals 1⁄16 ft.) times 150 fpm. A typical load of 4/4 wood in my kiln has 14 layers x 8.5 ft. x 1⁄16 ft. x 150 fpm, which equals approximately 1,100 cfm. The fan is mounted high so it can push the hot air down through the stack (Fig. A, page 100).

Roof angle is important. Determine your latitude; then use that latitude number, plus or minus 5 degrees, for the kiln roof's pitch. In Minnesota, for example, our latitude is about 45 degrees north, so I mounted the solar panel at a 45-degree angle.

Can I Air-Dry Wood Indoors?

Q: I have some cherry that's been dried outside for two years. Can I finish the drying process indoors?

A: Yes, you can. Even if your wood has been drying in Uncle Joe's barn for the past 100 years, the moisture content (MC) will be more than 15 percent. What you need is a MC of about 8 percent.

You can dry 4/4 lumber indoors from 15 percent to 8 percent in a single heating season. Remember, you don't have to bring in the whole stack at once. Just bring in enough to satisfy your needs for the coming year. I've had small stacks of wood drying in the attic, the basement and the garage. (In my experience, don't even think about the living room!)

If your basement is a bit damp in the summer, you can try running a dehumidifier or wait for winter when the basement is drier. If the wood seems to be drying too slowly, boost

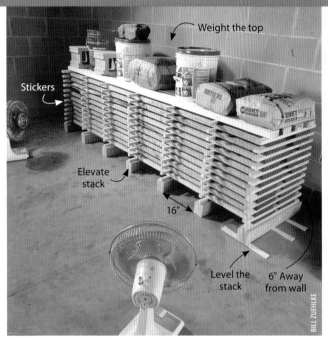

Weight the top

Stickers

Elevate stack

16"

Level the stack

6" Away from wall

the airflow by directing a fan or two at the pile.

Finally, buy an inexpensive moisture meter so you can tell exactly when your wood is ready to use.

ART DIRECTION: VERN JOHNSON • LEAD PHOTO: RAMON MORENO, ALL OTHERS: STAFF, UNLESS OTHERWISE INDICATED

Very Special Wood

N ever mind saving money, never mind the satisfaction, when you take control of finding and preparing your own wood, you'll become free to work with material that commercial sources consider too small, too gnarly, and too finicky. You'll have access to beautiful wood that can't be bought at any price. This chapter includes information about:

- spalted wood, which occurs when wood-eating micro-organisms colonize the log. If you can get to the wood before they complete their meal, you may find it written over with fantastic networks of black lines, like the beautiful bowl shown here.

- curly wood, which results from wavy grain inside the tree trunk. Nobody really knows why it occurs, and few woodworkers know how to work with it effectively. But you will know, after you study Tom Caspar's account on page 114.

- domestic woods like cherry, butternut, birch and mesquite, three undervalued commercial species that rival expensive exotics in their rich color and figure, and really come alive in the hands of a skilled woodworker.

- taming the bizarre grain of birdseye maple and finishing it to a high sparkle;

- finding your way around the inexpensive mahogany look-alikes that often appear on the commercial wood market.

❮ **Spalted birch burl bowl**
*by Mark Lindquist, 1987.
Collection of Arthur and
Jane Mason.*

by ALAN LACER

Spalted Wood

MOTHER NATURE DRAWS THESE BLACK LINES

Spalting is a by-product of the rotting process that is carried out by a vast army of stain, mold, and decay fungi. They are abundantly present in the air and soil, waiting for favorable conditions and a suitable host. Generally, wood moisture content of at least 25 percent, temperatures from about 40- to 90-degrees F, air, and food (especially abundant in sap wood) are what the fungi need. A tree or branch freshly fallen onto a damp forest floor in warm weather is asking for it.

Lighter colored woods offer the best canvas for nature's graphic work. Hard maple is viewed as the king of spalted woods, although sycamore, persimmon, red and white oak, elm, pecan, birch, buckeye, apple, magnolia, beech, holly, hackberry, box elder and the sapwoods of walnut and cocobolo are favored by woodworkers as well.

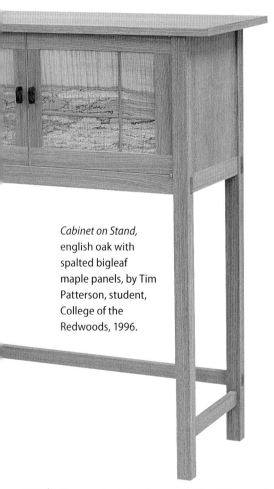

Cabinet on Stand, english oak with spalted bigleaf maple panels, by Tim Patterson, student, College of the Redwoods, 1996.

Where to Find Spalted Wood

You can purchase spalted wood—usually maple—from specialty lumber and mail order suppliers. Turning blocks are most easily found, but a few suppliers offer boards when they can get them.

Hunting spalted wood is like panning for gold—lots of searching for that one precious nugget. Logs rotting on the forest floor, dead limbs and entire dead standing trees are excellent sources. You can also hunt for hidden treasure at a community bone yard of removed trees, and don't overlook the bottom of your old firewood pile.

Make Your Own Spalted Wood

Woodworkers commonly use these methods to cause wood to spalt. They will work most effectively if the temperature is kept where the fungi will thrive, between 60- and 80-degrees F. Monitor the spalting progress monthly—the optimal conditions you've created can make it happen fast.

- Place a freshly cut log section 2 to 3 ft. long upright on the bare ground. Put a shovel of dirt on the top end and cover it loosely with black plastic.

- Bury a log, freshly sawn green boards or green rough-turned bowls in damp sawdust containing pieces of rotten wood with active fungi. Keep the sawdust moist.

- Use plastic bags or plastic garbage cans to hold short sections of green wood or rough-turned bowls. Adding some soil or rotting sawdust may speed the process, although the fungi already present in the air or on the wood surface is probably enough to get it going. Leave the bags or cans with a small opening to allow for some air exchange.

How to Stabilize Spalted Wood

Remove those things the fungi need to grow, and you'll stop its progress. One method is to lower the wood's moisture content. Wood below 25-percent moisture content, when kept in low relative humidity, is not likely to decay or even stain. Accomplish this by air or

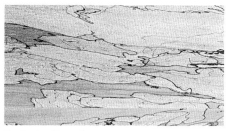
Spalted soft maple

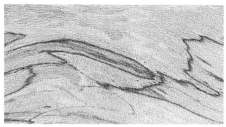
Spalted sycamore

Spalted holly (end-grain view)

kiln drying, placing smaller pieces in a microwave or finish turning if the piece was a rough-turned bowl. You can also raise or lower the wood's temperature. Spalting rarely occurs above 90-degrees F and stops below 32-degrees F. Some turners store blanks in a freezer prior to finish turning. Finally, you can restrict the air—no air, no decay. Logs submerged in water, for example, do not decompose from fungi. Tightly wrapping the wood in several layers of plastic will restrict the air and slow the growth of the fungi.

EDITOR: TIM JOHNSON • ART DIRECTION: MELANIE HAUBRICH • PHOTOGRAPHY: KRIVIT PHOTOGRAPHY • TECHNICAL ASSISTANCE: DR. ROBERT BLANCHETTE, UNIVERSITY OF MINNESOTA

Working Spalted Wood Safely

There is anecdotal and some medical evidence that substances from decaying wood are a health threat. Allergic reactions and some serious lung diseases have been traced to spores and fungi that inhabit rotting wood. The effect on an individual woodworker depends on his or her tolerance to the spores and fungi, the concentration of them in the environment and the length of exposure. Persons with weakened immune systems, lung illnesses or who show signs of allergic reactions to the spalted wood should avoid the material altogether. One must err on the side of caution when working spalted wood. Freshly sawn green material with active spores and fungi, or even air-dried material, is potentially the most hazardous. Kiln drying, by turning up the heat and driving out the moisture, will actually kill both fungi and spores. To avoid breathing spalted wood dust, I strongly recommend that you wear a respirator—not a nuisance mask—and have an effective point-of-origin dust collection system or a self-contained air filtration helmet. Avoid prolonged contact with your skin, and clean your work area thoroughly following any work with spalted wood.

Working Properties

If you're lucky, you'll catch the spalting at the right time, before the cellular structure of the wood deteriorates, and you'll be able to work the piece without any trouble. Sometimes, however, the material will have areas that have become soft and punky. These areas have no strength and defy normal woodworking strategies. They will crumble, tear out in chunks or leave a wrinkled appearance when you try to cut or plane them. They refuse to be glued together, and leave you with a cratered, uneven surface when you try to sand. Though not suitable for joinery, these soft areas can often be stiffened enough to finish so the piece of wood can still be used decoratively.

You can saturate soft areas with a liquid hardener. Where the wood is only marginally soft, a spot coat or two of clear shellac or nitrocellulose sanding sealer may harden it sufficiently. A really punky spot will require cyanoacrylate (CA) glue (the thin, watery type) or a product made to stabilize rotten wood. There are a number of them sold as wood hardeners at hardware stores. It may take several generous applications to treat each bad spot. These hardeners are effective, but they have side effects. They fill the wood cells, so surfaces treated with them can't be glued and oil

Worm-spalted red maple bowl by Alan Lacer, 1998. Typical spalting differs from worm spalt, where the worm hole allows the fungus to enter and work from the inside out.

Zone lines

An active fungus colony surrounds itself with a chemical and physical barrier that defines its outer boundaries. Filaments of the fungus pack and swell in these regions and exude generous amounts of pigmented material that usually appear as black lines. The material in these "zone lines" protects the colony from attack by bacteria, insects, and other fungi, and assists in maintaining a desirably moist atmosphere. Inset: Electron microscope view of a fungus zone line in front of wood cell structures.

finishes don't take well because they can't penetrate. Solvent-based hardeners and CA glues darken the wood considerably. I like Protective Coatings Petrifier. It's a water-based hardener that doesn't discolor the wood, yet seals and stiffens effectively. It's an excellent choice for troublesome soft spots.

You should be able to work the stiffened surface with edge tools—make very light cuts—or with abrasives, taking care to provide a firm, flat backing for the sandpaper. Some turners use body grinders or stiff-backed sanding discs and work the piece while it's spinning on the lathe. For flat lumber, an abrasive planer is an excellent option, followed by a random-orbit or pad sander. If you sand by hand, use a sanding block to give firm support to the paper.

Finishing

You are likely to encounter three problems when you finish spalted wood: Splotching, yellowing and excessive darkening. The whiter woods—which usually have the most dramatic examples of spalting—can turn quite yellow with certain finishes, and because the soft areas act like end-grain or even a sponge, splotching or excessive darkening can result unless the piece is sealed first.

An effective weapon against splotching is clear, dewaxed shellac used as a sealer. (Spray cans of shellac are thinned and dewaxed.) Cover the entire piece with a thin coat and let it dry. Then recoat dull-looking areas until all surfaces have a uniform sheen. You can use almost any finish as a topcoat over dewaxed shellac after it's been sanded.

To minimize yellowing and darkening, use a surface-film finish like clear shellac or lacquer. Waterborne finishes dry clear and don't yellow with age. If the piece is primarily decorative, clear wax is appropriate.

If you don't mind the yellowing and darkening, use your favorite oil finish, but be prepared to make many applications to the softer areas. An oil-finished spalted piece will appear muddy and uneven at first, but will look better as the finish cures, which can take weeks or even months.

If you are looking for a challenge, and effects that often surpass the wildest woods from the tropics, spalted wood may be your ticket. Use spalted wood and your work will never go unnoticed. Use it well, and you'll produce a real showstopper.

by TOM CASPAR

Curly Wood

HOW TO BUY, MACHINE, AND FINISH THIS AMAZING WOOD

Hidden within a few trees in every forest lies a mysteriously distorted wood that has always fascinated woodworkers.

You can't spot curly wood from the outside, but inside the tree a peculiar switch has been flipped, turning straight tree cells into wavy cells. Cut the tree open, plane the wood and you get spectacular, three-dimensional rippling wood grain.

But beauty comes at a price. You can tear your hair out trying to tame this unruly wood. Here are some practical tips on how to buy, machine, and finish curly wood.

What Is Curly Wood?

The stripes you see in a finished board of curly wood come from the play of light on grain that waves from side to side (Photo 1). The troughs and crests of the waves reflect light in different directions. As you turn a curly board around in your hands, its surface actually shimmers. Light areas turn dark and dark areas turn light.

The biology of curly wood is as mysterious as its appearance. No one really understands why some trees have this wavy grain. It's not genetic. You can take seeds from a curly tree, plant them

Curly white oak

Striped figure

Wavy grain

1 Split open a curly log and you'll find grain that bends back and forth like a wave. Planing the wood cuts through the waves, producing a shimmering effect like light bouncing off the ripples on a pond. This chunk of white oak is spectacular-looking wood!

ART DIRECTION: PATRICK HUNTER • PHOTOGRAPHY: STAFF UNLESS OTHERWISE INDICATED near their parent and get nothing but straight-grained timber. The best guess is that stressful growing conditions, such as cold and drought, turn on the curly switch in a few trees, but no one has figured out how to duplicate these conditions in order to grow curly trees.

Curly grain can appear and disappear within a single tree. One side of a tree can be curly, and the other side straight. Young outer layers may be curly, but not older inner layers. It's totally baffling!

Buying Curly Wood

Any kind of tree can become curly, but some species that grow in tough northern climates produce a greater percentage of curly wood than others (Photo 2). Flame birch and tiger maple are well-known examples, but you can uncover curly walnut, curly cherry, and curly oak, just to name a few.

If you're lucky, you can find curly wood in any pile of lumber for the same price as a straight-grained board. Many lumber mills process logs so fast they don't stop and cull the unusual curly ones. If you search for curly boards in the rough, look for a striped barber-pole surface or alternating areas of smooth and fuzzy grain.

A few folks in the lumber trade make it their business to find curly logs. Wood prospectors mine for curly gold in the hundreds of average trees felled by a lumber mill. The prospectors peel back the bark of some logs before they're sawn. If they hit pay dirt, they'll purchase the log and gamble that most of it is truly curly. No one will really know how spectacular or faint the curl is until it's sawn.

Each dealer has their own system of grading curly wood, based both on general figure and the number of curls per inch. They'll be the first to tell you that curly wood is so unusual that it defies classification. Your best bet for consistency is to stick with a dealer who has a large stockpile and familiarity with this enigmatic wood.

The Benefits of Wide Boards

Many dealers in curly wood hoard wide stock. Their logs are custom sawn to maximize the width of each board.

Why go to so much trouble? Imagine a drawer front made of three curly boards glued together. Individually, each board looks fantastic, but they don't work together (photo 3, page 116). One wide board for the drawer front would look much better. Experienced builders of reproduction furniture look high and low for wide boards.

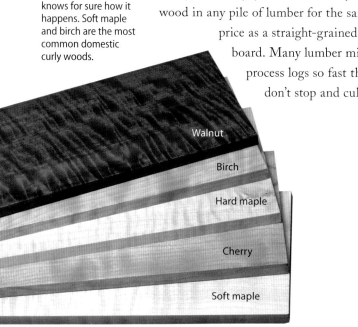

2 Curly wood is found in every kind of tree under the sun. Environmental factors probably turn normal trees into curly ones, but nobody knows for sure how it happens. Soft maple and birch are the most common domestic curly woods.

Walnut

Birch

Hard maple

Cherry

Soft maple

Bookmatching

If you resaw and bookmatch curly wood, light can play tricks on you (photo 4). Sure, you've made a wide board with mirror-image grain (the physical structure of the cells), but look what happens to the figure (the surface appearance of the cells). The grain runs uphill on one side of the board and downhill on the other.

What does that do to the figure? One side of the board can be light, the other side dark. Shift your viewpoint and the brightness shifts the other way. Again, a wide board may be a better choice. Musical instrument makers routinely bookmatch the curly wood they call fiddleback maple, but they're awfully picky about selecting just the right boards.

Reducing Tear-Out

Curly boards are notoriously difficult to joint and plane, but armed with some woodworking savvy you can usually produce a blemish-free surface. The problem is the grain, which changes direction with every ripple (photo 5). It runs downhill on one side of a wave and uphill on the other side. So no matter which way you feed a board, whole hunks of wood can be yanked off the surface by a machine's knives, leaving an ugly pit behind. If you've just spent a pile of money on some special wood, this can be heartbreaking. Here's how to minimize tear-out:

- Change your knives. Dull knives on a jointer or planer pull on wood grain; sharp knives cut it cleanly.
- Take a light cut. Set your machine to remove ¹⁄₆₄ to ¹⁄₃₂ in. at a time. Sure,

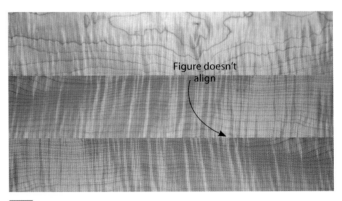

3 Glued-up curly boards may not go well together. Curly figure is unusual because it runs at right angles to the edge of a board. It's difficult to align figure like this in a group of narrow boards. Instead, look for wide boards.

Figure doesn't align

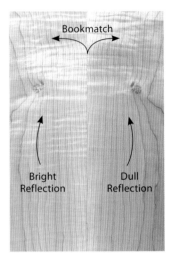

4 Resawing a curly board into two bookmatched pieces makes a wide panel, but you may not like what you see. Although the grain structure is the same in both boards, the figure doesn't look the same. Bright areas on one side may look like dull areas on the other side.

Bookmatch

Bright Reflection　　*Dull Reflection*

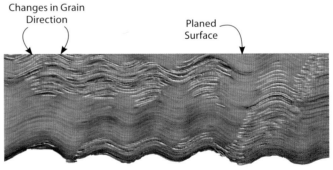

Changes in Grain Direction　　*Planed Surface*

5 The planed surface of a curly board slices right through the waves of grain. Making a curly surface smooth and free of tear-out is pretty tricky, because the grain constantly changes direction. Half the time you're actually cutting against the grain!

6 Wetting the surface of curly wood before jointing or planing virtually eliminates tear-out. This may be hard to believe, but temporarily softening the fibers really works!

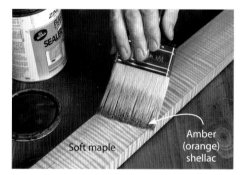

7 Finishes that are slightly colored emphasize the curls more than perfectly clear finishes. Amber shellac has an extra amount of color, enhancing the effect.

8 Dye penetrates deeply into the thirsty end-grain areas of the curls. It makes them stand out from the surrounding wood. For even more contrast, sand the board. The curls remain dark while the surrounding wood stays light. Then, apply a second coat of dye.

you'll take many more passes, but you'll minimize the depth of any tear-out.

- Wet the wood. Green wood is easier to cut than dried wood, because wet cells are easier to separate and less likely to pry out their neighbors. You can temporarily achieve the same effect on kiln-dried wood by lightly sponging the surface of a board before you joint or plane (photo 6). Give your jointer bed a good waxing and the board won't drag. Rest assured, you won't rust your cutter heads as long as you clean and dry them right away.

- Feed slowly. Go slow on the jointer, about half the speed you normally use.

- Scrape, don't plane. If you're working with hand tools, use a No. 80 scraper plane. Its steep cutting angle allows you to quickly remove milling marks without any fear of tear-out. A card scraper is the perfect tool for smoothing small areas of shallow tear-out.

Despite your best efforts, a little tear-out when working curly wood is inevitable. Don't get too discouraged. Some curly boards are so wild that even the finest woodworkers turn to two more tools: drum sanders and putty. A drum sander is a surefire (and expensive) way to surface curly wood perfectly smooth. It's slower than a jointer or planer, but you're guaranteed a clean shave. For tiny pits of tear-out that run pretty deep, use putty. If you scrape or sand down to the bottom of the tear-out you might end up creating a whole new problem: a shallow, dished out divot. You may not see it right away, but it'll show up under a finish.

Finishing Tips

The amount of color in a finish can make a big difference in bringing out the curl. The explanation lies in looking once more at curly wood's grain structure. Remember how the surface of a flat board cuts right through the rising and falling grain? When the grain rises up to the surface it exposes the ends of many cells. These end-grain cells are thirsty to absorb a finish, just like the end grain of any board. But the side-grain cells on the crests and troughs of each wave don't absorb as much finish. The result is that some areas of a board soak up more finish (and color) than others.

Finishes such as shellac, oil, and varnish are slightly colored. The thirsty parts of a board soak up an extra amount of this color. This extra color really makes the curl pop. Orange or amber shellac has more color than blond shellac, making the effect particularly striking (photo 7, page 117).

Other finishes such as lacquer and waterborne polyurethane don't have much color in them. You can still see the curl under them, but it's not as dramatic. However, if you apply these finishes over a coat of dewaxed shellac you can have the best of both worlds.

Dyeing Curly Figure

Here's a neat trick using dyes instead of stains to emphasize the dark figure of curls. This is a shop-tested recipe to simulate the look of antique curly maple furniture:

1. Sand your maple to 220 grit and apply one coat of Dark Mission Brown water-soluble dye, mixed ⅛ tsp. powder to 1 cup water. Let dry.

2. Re-sand with 220 grit paper. Sand until the wood surrounding the dark-colored curls is light.

3. Apply Early American water-soluble dye mixed ½ tsp. powder to 1 cup water. Let dry.

4. Apply a liberal amount of boiled linseed oil. Wipe off the excess after 30 minutes. Let dry at least three days.

5. To further warm the color of the wood and give it an aged look, apply a burnt umber glaze.

6. Apply your favorite topcoat. If you're using a waterborne finish, apply dewaxed shellac first.

ART DIRECTION: VERN JOHNSON • PHOTOGRAPHY: PAGE 62, THOS. MOSER, CHRONICLE BOOKS, 2002 (OTU); OTHER PAGES, PATRICK HUNTER UNLESS NOTED

by TOM CASPAR

The Magic of Cherry

NO WOOD CAN RIVAL THE DEPTH AND COMPLEXITY OF CHERRY'S COLOR AND FIGURE

I'm sitting at a figured-cherry writing desk I built more than 20 years ago. I intimately know every square inch, but when my eyes wander from my laptop computer to the wood, it always captures my imagination. What is it about old cherry that's so endlessly fascinating? Cherry is surprisingly bland when freshly planed, but after a few years, it glows like the embers of a warm, comforting campfire. To make that magic happen doesn't require smoke and mirrors, though, just smart purchasing and shrewd woodworking skills.

Cherry's Allure

For my home, dark walnut is too formal, light maple too stark. I prefer working with American hardwoods rather than imported species, so when I want a medium-toned wood to relax with in my home, I build with cherry. It's fairly easy to work, like walnut or red oak, but the real appeal for me is its rich appearance.

Age Improves Color

The real beauty of cherry takes time to mature. Cherry is a uniform pale salmon color when first cut, but over the course of a year or so, its surface slowly turns to a dark auburn set against a golden background. It is possible to stain or chemically treat a brand-new project so it looks somewhat like this deep color, but your best bet is simply to use a clear finish and be patient. As with aging a fine wine, let nature do its work.

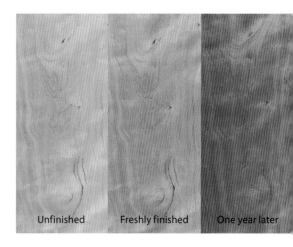

Unfinished   Freshly finished   One year later

Exceptional Curly Figure

Curly figure is quite common in cherry. As you walk around a figured board, the dark areas turn light and the light areas go dark, just like the luster of fine silk. Even a small amount of subtle curly figure under a clear finish can make magic. This stunning 3-D effect is called chatoyancy. Large-scale lumber dealers generally don't separate curly from straight-grained boards. When lumberyard boards are planed hit-or-miss, you can easily spot the curly wood. With some practice you can even spot chatoyancy in rough, unplaned lumber. Just look for dark ripples that go across the width of the board.

Beware the Phantom

Cherry needs unobstructed exposure to light and air to turn color evenly. Don't leave a lamp, book or other solid object on top of your cherry furniture for an extended length of time during its first year. The wood underneath the object won't darken as fast, which results in a light-colored phantom "shadow" that may never completely disappear.

This problem starts when you first plane rough cherry boards. After planing, if you leave them piled willy-nilly overnight, you'll get shadow lines where they overlapped. At the end of a day's work, I stand all my boards on edge, separated from one another, so all faces get equal exposure to light and air.

Matching Color and Figure

The biggest challenge in working with cherry is to select boards that harmoniously blend with each other. I've spent hours at a lumberyard picking through piles of cherry, looking for the right family of boards, and the extra time is worth it.

Stain

Choose Carefully, Don't Stain

Cherry boards come in many shades. I look for boards that are similar in color and figure so I can use a clear finish and let the wood change color naturally. Many nonwoodworkers assume cherry is very dark and has little or no figure. That's because most commercial cherry furniture is stained or toned to even out color differences and blend in light-colored sapwood. I understand the economics of this practice, but in my small shop, I consider stain a last resort. It simply obscures the magic.

Buy a Log

Some custom sawmills go to a lot of trouble to restack whole logs after they've been cut and dried (see Sources, page 204). This is a gold mine for cherry prospectors. Naturally, this wood will cost a bit more. Most custom mills have a $300 or so minimum order. You can buy an entire log (often called a flitch) or neighboring boards, depending on the mill's sales policy. Keep in mind that all the wood in a log won't necessarily be the highest grade. Some boards may have knots and checks. To avoid any misunderstandings, it's best to phone in rather than e-mail an order.

Saw a Giant Board

When it comes to matching color and figure, the next best thing to buying a cut-up log is to saw one yourself. You don't need a sawmill in your backyard, just a good bandsaw. Look for the longest, widest, thickest cherry board you can find. For a project requiring a modest amount of solid wood, you might get all the parts from one humongous board. Maybe it'll take two monsters. For maximum yield, rip and resaw the board before planing.

MIKE HABERMANN

"All-red" board

Sapwood

Smart Buying

Whether you're visiting a local lumberyard or ordering cherry by phone, you've got to know the wood and keep up with the lingo. I was recently surprised to learn that you can buy a super-premium grade of cherry if you know what to ask for.

The "All-Red" Grade

Be on the alert for light-colored sapwood when you select cherry boards. It's a dramatically different color than the heartwood. It's perfectly OK to have sapwood on the hidden, inside face of your boards, but sapwood on the outside face can be very hard to disguise.

Sapwood isn't considered a defect when most cherry is graded. That means Select and Better cherry boards, the highest standard grade, may well contain lots of sapwood, or none at all.

Some lumber dealers select cherry boards that have little or no sapwood and sell them at a premium price. They might be labeled as "all-red" or some variation of that phrase. This is a grade that has not been standardized nationally, so the percentage of sapwood allowed varies from dealer to dealer.

Lower Grade = Savings

Prime cherry costs from $5 to $9 per bd. ft. Only a small percentage is designated as the highest Select and Better grade. Grading is based on minimum widths and lengths and a low incidence of knots. No. 1 Common is a lower, less-expensive grade, and there's plenty available. You just have to plan around the knots or glue narrow boards to make wide ones.

Watch Out for Gum Pockets

Gum pockets are small black streaks that form under the bark. Gum pockets can mar the appearance of an otherwise gorgeous board. On the other hand, placed judiciously, gum pockets can add character to an otherwise plain surface. Look for gum pockets before you cut full-size boards.

Pennsylvania Grows the Best

Although good-looking cherry grows throughout the Eastern United States, wood from the Allegheny Plateau in northwestern

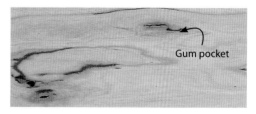

Gum pocket

Pennsylvania has a national reputation for being a more uniform, richer red color than cherry from other regions.

by TIM JOHNSON

Butternut

TIPS FOR WORKING WITH BLACK WALNUT'S BLOND COUSIN

Butternut is one of our prettiest domestic hardwoods, but most people have never seen it. Butternut trees are rare in urban and suburban landscapes, and retail lumberyards don't usually stock it. Even though furniture makers and carvers have valued it for centuries, butternut lumber has never been commercially important.

It's easy to mistake butternut for another wood. With a natural finish, it can look like oak, or even birch. Stained brown, butternut is a dead ringer for black walnut. Shaker cabinetmakers colored it with washes of blue, green, red and yellow. Woodcarvers love butternut, but you're more likely to admire their handiwork than the wood from which it springs.

Butternut lumber is affordable, beautiful and enjoyable to work with, and the trees are valuable members of our forests. Sadly, a deadly fungus is ravaging them. Our generation may be the last with an opportunity to get to know this great American hardwood.

Black Walnut's Cousin

A member of the walnut family, butternut (Juglans cinerea) is often referred to as "white walnut," because of its light tan to cinnamon-colored heartwood (Photo 1). Fresh-cut boards can have light and dark streaks, and pink, green, or gray hues. These tones disappear gradually over time, as do the dark-colored pores. Antiques made of butternut have turned a uniform golden color.

Butternut's plainsawn figure is nearly identical to black walnut's, although its "cathedrals" are more likely to be multi-spired (Photo 2). Butternut's texture is also similar to that of black walnut—more coarse than maple or cherry, but finer than ash or oak. The pores are visible, just like they are in black walnut.

Butternut grows from eastern Canada to Minnesota, through eastern Nebraska and as far south as Arkansas, Alabama and Georgia. Typically, it's found growing widely scattered in mixed hardwood stands.

butternut   walnut

1 Butternut looks just like black walnut, only lighter. Genetic cousins, their figure patterns are similar.

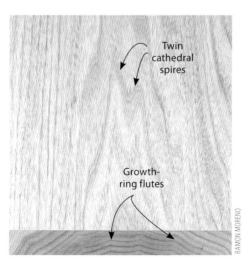

Twin cathedral spires

Growth-ring flutes

2 Fluted growth rings are characteristic. They give plainsawn butternut its unusual twin-spired cathedral figure.

Buying Butternut

Top-grade boards of 4/4 (1-in. thick) rough stock cost about $4 per bd. ft. Typical boards are 6 to 8-ft. long and about 7-in. wide. You may even find some really wide ones, over 12 inches. Wild-looking grain is common in butternut. You'll find knots and other defects too, even in top-grade boards. Lower-grade No. 1 common boards cost around $3 per bd. ft. The biggest commercial use of butternut is to make paneling, using the lower grades.

If your local hardwood lumberyard doesn't stock butternut, dig a little deeper. Check the Yellow Pages or your local woodworker's group to find nearby sawmills and other small-scale lumber suppliers. These operations are likely to handle a variety of locally-available hardwoods. If you live within butternut's native range, you might hit the jackpot. You can also find butternut on the Web. A good place to start is WoodFinder at *www.wdfindr.com.*

Working with Butternut

Butternut is much softer than walnut and not nearly as strong. It dents so easily you can mark it with a fingernail (Photo 3). It isn't a good choice for a fine tabletop, but it's perfect if you want a distressed country look.

Butternut is also easy to move around. A 12-in.-wide, 10-ft.-long plank of kiln-dried 4/4 stock weighs only about 20 lb. A similar-size walnut plank weighs well over 30 lb.

The best working characteristic of butternut is the way it responds to hand-held edge tools, as long as their cutting edges are kept razor-sharp. It's no secret why butternut was popular with pioneer woodworkers. It cuts easily, planes beautifully and carves like butter (Photos 4 and 5). If you want to try hand-planing, a great place to start is with a straight-grained piece of butternut.

Ironically, machine tools can bring out the worst in butternut. This is one reason butternut isn't used commercially. Surface-planing or edge-routing can tear the soft fibers from the surface without warning, leaving it fuzzy (Photo 6). The torn fibers are hard to deal with. They're so stringy, you can actually peel them away from the surface, leaving unsightly channels. Planing by hand with a razor-sharp tool is the best way to remove them. It's tough to sand torn fibers smooth. They either crush because they're so soft, or tear because they're so stringy.

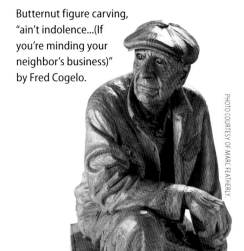

Butternut figure carving, "ain't indolence...(If you're minding your neighbor's business)" by Fred Cogelo.

PHOTO COURTESY OF MARC FEATHERLY

Butternut is too soft for a tabletop, unless you want to get a distressed look very quickly! Even though it's a hardwood, butternut is as soft as white pine.

Butternut planes easily by hand, which is one reason it was favored by 19th-century woodworkers.

Butternut is great for carving because its end grain and face grain are equally hard. It cuts easily and holds a crisp edge.

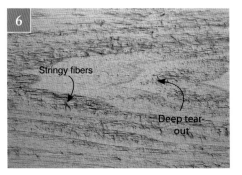

Stringy fibers

Deep tear-out

Machining can cause stringy tear-out that's difficult to remove.

Use a sanding block to keep the surface level when you sand. Sand with fine paper only and replace it often.

Sanding Butternut

Butternut is so soft, it's important not to go overboard when you sand. Always use fine-grit sandpaper. Anything below 150 grit will tear the soft fibers. So will dull, worn-out grit. Don't sand a torn-out spot with finger pressure. You'll just create a divot. Instead, use a sanding block. Be careful when you use a random-orbit sander. Use fine paper and go easy.

I prefer to sand butternut by hand, with a good old cork-faced sanding block (Photo 7), starting with 180 grit. After 180, I go to 220 and finish off with 280 grit.

Finishing Butternut

Shellac and butternut go together like a hand in a glove (lead photo, page 124). If you're stuck with some fuzziness that you just can't sand out, a wash coat of dewaxed shellac stiffens the fuzzy fibers and gives you another chance to sand them smooth before applying your finish coats. For a deeper amber tone, or really troublesome fuzz, apply and sand down a second wash coat.

Butternut stains like it sands—almost too well. If you don't have the surface sanded uniformly, or if you've got some fuzzy spots, stains can look blotchy. I get the best-looking results when I use a wood conditioner prior to staining (Photo 8).

Conditioner applied first

Make butternut look like walnut with oil stain. Stain alone will make it really dark, because the wood is so porous. It's best to start with a wood conditioner.

Heartwood

Sapwood

Up to 40 percent of a birch log is light-colored sapwood.

by TIM JOHNSON

Birch

THIS AFFORDABLE WOOD IS GREAT FOR BOTH HIGH-END AND UTILITARIAN CABINETRY

ART DIRECTION: PATRICK HUNTER · PHOTOGRAPHY: STAFF, UNLESS OTHERWISE INDICATED

Birch is a hot item at the lumberyard these days, and birch veneer is the all-time most popular hardwood plywood. This isn't a fad. Despite changes in taste and fashion, birch has been in demand for furniture and cabinetry for almost a century.

Birch lumber has a handsome appearance. Because of its fine texture and straight grain, it machines well and routs beautifully. Though hard, birch is easy to sand, and it turns like a dream. Birch plywood is available in a wide range of grades.

These characteristics make birch a great choice for all types of cabinetry. But the best thing about birch is that it looks good with a variety of finishes— it's a great impostor for more expensive woods. I'll show you how to make the most of this durable, versatile and budget-friendly hardwood.

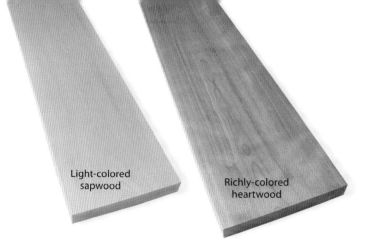

Light-colored sapwood

Richly-colored heartwood

Birch is famous for its light-colored sapwood, but its deeper-toned heartwood, which is known as red birch in the lumber industry, can be even more appealing.

Birch Lumber is Graded for Color

Birch logs contain quite a bit of sapwood. It ranges in color from creamy-white to golden tan (with occasional pink tones), and is distinctly different than the reddish-brown heartwood (photo, at left). Commercial demand for light-colored wood is so strong that birch, like maple, is often graded and sold by its color. You'll pay about a 20-percent premium for color-selected birch.

At the lumberyard, birch boards marketed as "sap" or "white" have been color-selected. Sap birch refers to boards containing at least 85 percent light-colored sapwood. White birch refers to paper birch. Some lumberyards carry it separately from yellow birch, specifically for its white color. Paper birch boards are usually narrow (about 4-in. wide), short (6- to 8-ft. long) and thin (1-in. thick). They're best used to make face-frames and moldings.

Most birch lumber is sold as natural or unselected. There's no difference in the quality of the wood—it just hasn't been sorted for color. Most natural boards contain a combination of sapwood and heartwood, but you'll find light- and dark-colored boards as part of the mix. While light-colored birch grabs all the attention, its deeper toned heartwood (red birch) can be just as attractive. Thick stock (over 1 in.) is likely to contain considerable heartwood. Lower-grade No. 1 common birch lumber contains more knots and other natural defects.

Yellow Birch Rules

Although the birch family Betulaceae contains over a dozen domestic species, between 80 and 90 percent of the lumber you'll find at the lumberyard is yellow birch (Betula alleghaniensis). Three other species are also commercially harvested and may occasionally be mixed in with yellow birch. Paper birch (B. papyrifera) is whiter, but softer. Sweet birch (B. lenta) is a bit harder and has a deeper color. River birch (B. nigra) is more likely to contain knots. Birch boards average about 6-in. wide, and are available in lengths up to 12 ft. Lumberyards usually stock birch in 1- and 2-in. thicknesses. Home centers carry birch plywood, but may not stock birch lumber.

VESSEL BY RUS HURT

Birch burl is prized by turners.

Yellow birch

Cherry

Mahogany

Walnut

Birch is a great impostor because its figure patterns closely resemble those in cherry, mahogany and walnut. You can dress it up or down just by staining it different colors. Furniture manufacturers have used stained birch in lieu of more expensive hardwoods for decades.

Birch Plywood Has Many Faces

Birch plywood is graded by its color, just like birch lumber. The highest grade is white, followed by uniform light and natural. Lower paint and shop grades cost less. Hardwood lumberyards usually stock most grades.

The faces of white birch ply (here white refers to color, rather than species) are made of top-grade (zero defects), color-matched sapwood veneers. This architectural-quality plywood has a handsome appearance, but it's expensive; around $75 per sheet.

Uniform light and natural birch ply have top-grade veneer faces, in terms of natural defects, but they're not pristinely white in color. In the past, these grades were distinctly different. Today, they're virtually identical in appearance (they're both light colored) and in price; about ten percent less than white ply. Paint and shop grades of birch plywood are worth looking at if you want to save money. They cost about

$50 per sheet. Paint-grade birch ply has face veneers that vary in color and pattern match. Shop-grade sheets have some kind of damage or manufacturing defect, but must be 85 percent usable.

White birch plywood

Top grades of birch plywood are white and uniform. They're the best choice if you want a clean, pristine look.

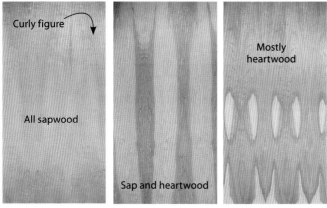

Curly figure

All sapwood

Sap and heartwood

Mostly heartwood

Middle-grade birch plywood sold at home centers offers lots of creative possibilities. The veneers may show attractive figure patterns, occasional spectacular curly figure, rich colors, and any combination of sap- and heartwood, including all of one or the other. Staining will minimize contrasting colors, but the only way to make these sheets white is to paint them!

It's smart to shop for birch plywood at a home center. They typically stock a mid-level grade, similar to the paint grade at the hardwood lumberyard, but at home center prices. This plywood will vary widely in appearance from sheet to sheet, and will contain minor natural defects, varying amounts of heartwood and slightly less uniform core material, but you'll save up to 50 percent, compared to the top white grades at the hardwood lumberyard. You'll also be able to look through the stack for the best-looking sheets. Take a friend along to help you look, be careful, and leave the stack neat for the next customer.

Birch or Hard Maple?

Yellow birch and hard maple look so much alike it's often tough to tell them apart. Plainsawn boards have similar figure patterns. They both have pale sapwood and distinctly darker heartwood. Manufacturers have used them interchangeably for decades.

How do they compare?

- Hard-maple sapwood is whiter.
- Hard maple will make a better cutting block or countertop, but yellow birch is tough enough to stand up to normal dings and dents.
- Both show considerable seasonal movement.
- Both yellow with age.
- Birch machines better. Hard maple is particularly prone to tear-out during edge jointing, and burn marks from dull blades and bits are tougher to remove.
- Birch accepts stain better, although both are prone to blotching.
- Birch costs less. Although demand for light-colored wood continues to push up the price of both species, birch is usually about 30-percent cheaper.

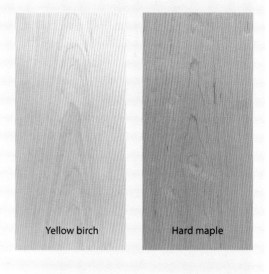

Yellow birch

Hard maple

Seal Birch Before You Stain

Curly figure is common in birch and occasionally it's spectacular. Flame birch can look as cool as tiger maple. Usually, though, figure is a big nuisance because it's randomly located and hard to see. If you're not careful, a piece with hidden curly figure can end up in the wrong place on your project. One curly board in a tabletop will stick out like a sore thumb, especially if you use stain. It's a good idea to check every board for figure. Just wipe on some mineral spirits; any figure will jump right out. If you're stuck with curly figure in the wrong place, using wood conditioner before you stain helps camouflage it.

Brush on water-based wood conditioner, let it dry and sand lightly before you stain. This process helps the wood absorb water-based stain evenly. Each coat of stain adds a little more color. You can tweak the color by using different colored stains, one over another. Water-based stains dry fast, so you can put on several coats in a day.

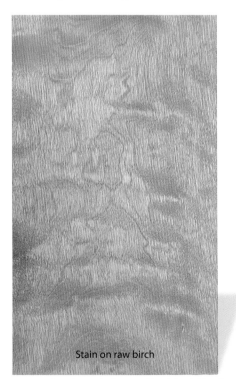

Stain on raw birch

Stain makes the curly figure of birch look blotchy.

Stain over conditioner

Curly figure is subdued when you apply water-based wood conditioner before you stain. In our experience, two coats of conditioner may be needed for best appearance.

Four Great Birch Finishes

Birch's chameleon-like nature makes it a finisher's dream wood. It looks good with a clear finish, accepts all colors of stains and dyes, and has a smooth surface that's great for painting.

Keep it light. Waterborne polyurethane adds no amber color, so it keeps birch as light as possible. Lacquer finishes are also clear. Oil-based finishes add an amber tone.

Imitate expensive hardwoods like mahogany, walnut or cherry. To simulate the open-pored appearance of mahogany or walnut, use a single coat of water-based conditioner before staining. You'll get an evenly colored finish and some stain will darken the pores, just like the real McCoy. To imitate close-pored woods like cherry, use two coats of conditioner. When you stain, the pores won't show up at all.

Match old birch cabinets or trim moldings that have aged to a uniform honey color by sealing new birch with two coats of water-based conditioner, just as if you were matching a close-pored wood. Then add color, using a golden-oak colored water-based stain.

Paint it. Because of its uniform texture and tiny pores, birch provides a smooth surface for painting. It's tougher than pine or poplar, and unselected grades cost about the same. For cabinetry, even the ugliest birch plywood will look great when it's painted.

by KEN E. ROGERS

Mesquite

RENEWABLE AMERICAN EXOTIC

Looking for a unique wood for a special project? Look no further than the short-bodied mesquite tree of the southwestern United States. Its swirling grain, variable color and numerous character defects—ring shake, ingrown bark, mineral streaks, borer holes and dormant buds—offer a treasure trove of hidden beauty for the woodworker.

Mesquite trees grow in abundance in the Southwest, and typically have a short trunk with many horizontal branches.

PHOTO BY KEN E. ROGERS

A Renewable Resource

Mesquite grows on more than eighty-two million acres in the southwestern United States, and on more than four times that much non-rain forest area in Mexico and South America. Mesquite trees sprout profusely from cut stumps, so the trees grow back naturally after harvesting. Mesquite grows like a weed, and has invaded nearly twenty-five million acres of rangeland over the past 50 years, becoming a nuisance for ranchers. Although the physical properties of mesquite are more like a rain forest tree, mesquite is clearly a renewable resource.

Exquisite Color, Exquisite Grain

Mesquite's dark, rich reddish brown wood rivals other fine native hardwoods such as walnut and cherry, and exotic species like rosewood, mahogany and cocobolo.

Mesquite's grain is open and fine-to-medium textured, rather like mahogany (although much harder). The wood is easy to work, despite its hardness, finishes smoothly, and polishes to a high, natural sheen. The sapwood is pale yellowish white in color and about ½ to 1-in. wide regardless of how big the board is. The heartwood ranges from dark yellowish brown, through shades of gray-brown to deep reddish, almost purple-brown.

One of the distinctive characteristics of mesquite is that, unlike many other dark woods, it doesn't get black, muddy or bleached with exposure to sunlight.

Mesquite is often dramatically figured, with crotch, bird's-eye and burl figure.

Mesquite wood typically ages to a uniform, warm, dark reddish brown with exposure to the sun's ultraviolet light (see Bowl, page 138).

Mesquite often has dramatic figure. There is feathered figure in wide and deep limb crotches where the grain figure from the limbs and trunk blend. Crotch wood is great for special projects such as pens, jewelry box tops and small wood turnings. A special treat is the crotch wood where three, four or more limbs come together.

Wood from mesquite's root-collar (at the ground line) has numerous, often hundreds, of dormant buds just under the bark, revealed as distinctive bird's eye figure. This is especially beautiful on the curved surfaces of turnings.

Burls are very common in mesquite, and present an additional source of highly figured wood. Mistletoe burls

EDITOR: KEN COLLIER • ART DIRECTION: PATRICK HUNTER • PHOTOGRAPHY: BILL ZUEHLKE, UNLESS OTHERWISE INDICATED • ILLUSTRATION: DON RAYMOND

Streaks

Ring shake

Mesquite has many character defects, in the form of splits, ring shakes (cracks that follow growth rings), bark inclusions, insect holes, and mineral streaks. These are an essential part of the character of this wood, and can be used to great aesthetic advantage.

Bark inclusion

grow at locations where a bird deposited a mistletoe seed on a limb, and as the mistletoe grew, it created havoc in the growth tissue of the tree. The result is a long, swollen burl. The highly irregular grain is great for lamps and natural-edged vessels. In some trees, the burl figure goes through the entire tree!

Defects are Common

You'll rarely find mesquite as clear boards or chunks. The wood is full of bark inclusions, mineral stains, insect holes and even the occasional grown-over rock. Particularly characteristic of mesquite is "ring shake" where the wood splits along a growth ring of the tree. Most woodworkers choose to take advantage of these defects by including them in their work, consolidating cracks and other problems with epoxy. Because of these defects, mesquite is most commonly used in turnings, sculpture and one-of-a-kind work where the defects add to the character of the piece.

Mesquite Boards are Short and Narrow

Mesquite trees have short trunks with lots of branches. Consequently, the lumber doesn't easily fit National Hardwood Lumber Association (NHLA) grading guidelines. Although an NHLA grading standard has been developed for mesquite, few sawmillers use it. If you tell a mesquite sawmiller, "I need eight or ten 12-ft. mesquite boards to build a large table," he'll probably tell you that he's been cutting mesquite for more than 20 years and has only seen a couple of boards near that size. With mesquite, the watchword is "short and narrow." A 2-in. x 6-in. x 6-ft.-long clear board is extremely rare.

Straight mesquite logs are typically 5 to 8-ft. long at most, and 15 to 18-in. in diameter. Longer and larger logs usually

Mesquite trees are small, so the boards are short and narrow. They are usually not graded by standard hardwood grades, but by appearance.

contain excessive ring shake or are too crooked to yield long, straight, clear lumber.

You should expect to pay $5 to $8 or more per bd. ft. of kiln-dried, surfaced lumber and $12 or more for premium boards with exceptional beauty. However, air-dried rough lumber is often all you'll be able to find.

Mesquite lumber is often graded into four general appearance grades:

- **Premium:** large size and fine figure
- **No. 1:** large size and/or much clear surface measure
- **No. 2:** average size and average clear surface measure ˌ
- **No. 3:** much defect with the integrity of the board compromised. This grade is usually cut up for small projects.

The rule when buying mesquite is to work closely with your supplier. Make sure they know what you want regarding size and color, because mesquite, with all its defects, is extremely variable.

Exceptional Stability

Mesquite is amazingly stable, completely unlike any other American species. Its maximum dimensional change due to fluctuations in moisture content is about one-fourth that of woods such as oak and walnut. And unlike most other woods, mesquite's dimensional change is about the same in both the radial and tangential directions (Fig. B). This means no cupping. A square of mesquite stays a square, and a circle stays a circle.

Fig. A Mesquite Doesn't Move Much

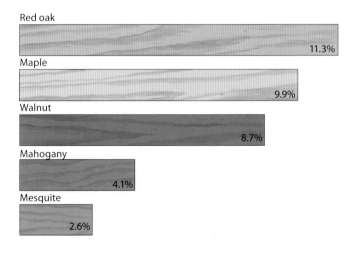

Mesquite expands and contracts much, much less than any common hardwood. These values represent the change in width of plain-sawn boards with a swing in moisture content from 6 to 14 percent.

Fig. B Mesquite Doesn't Distort

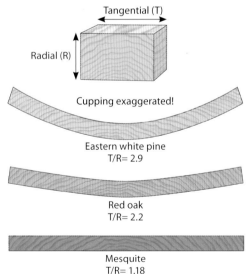

CUPPING is usually the result of plain-sawn boards shrinking more in the tangential direction than radially. In most American species, this ratio is more than 2 to 1. In mesquite, it's close to 1 to 1; so boards stay flat, a square stays a square and turnings stay cylindrical.

Tough, Hard and Easy to Finish

Mesquite's high silica content, high extractive content and extreme hardness can dull your tools quickly, especially if you force the wood through your saws and planers too fast. Start with sharp tools and resharpen about twice as often as usual. Wipe your saw blades occasionally with a solvent (like mineral spirits) to minimize extractive buildup. Unlike some dark, hard exotic species, mesquite does not have much natural oil, so it doesn't clog sandpaper and can be glued easily with standard glues.

Mesquite finishes well with many types of wood finishes. Because it's so hard, mesquite polishes beautifully with fine sanding grits and buffing, so often very little finish may be needed.

Prince of Turning Woods

Mesquite truly shines on the lathe. Its fantastic character marks and swirling fine-textured grain, along with its extreme stability and hardness, make mesquite a joy to turn. Green mesquite works like butter on the lathe, with long strings of curlings falling to the floor. The heat from sanding will dry the surface enough for you to put a finish on while the wood is still green. The wood dries nice and slowly (and without warping) through the finish.

Fig. C Mesquite Is Hard

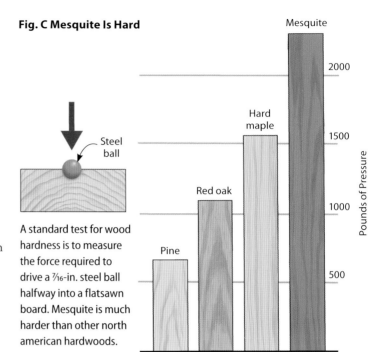

A standard test for wood hardness is to measure the force required to drive a ⁷⁄₁₆-in. steel ball halfway into a flatsawn board. Mesquite is much harder than other north american hardwoods.

VESSEL BY ALAN LACER

Mesquite shines as a turning wood, where its defects make for visual interest. It's also easy to cut when green and dries without distortion.

PHOTO BY KEN E.ROGERS

Watch out for the sapwood! Insects love it, especially when the wood is green, but also after you've built your project.

Sapwood

Avoid the Sapwood!

You'll be tempted to use mesquite's yellowish sapwood because of its attractive contrast with the dark heartwood. Don't! Wood-boring insects love the sapwood and are attracted to it immediately after the tree is felled. They also can infest your project's sapwood years later. It's heartbreaking to turn a fantastic vessel or make an exquisite jewelry box, only to later find little piles of yellow sawdust lying around its base.

Watch Out for the Dust

Some woodworkers have immediate allergic reactions to the chemical extractives in mesquite dust. Others develop the reaction over time. Always wear a face mask and use a dust collection system on your power tools. A few of my woodworker friends in Texas didn't take this concern seriously and they've had to give up woodworking because of allergies they developed over the years.

Save the Scraps for Your Barbecue!

When you work with mesquite, you get an added bonus. Waste, end cuts and even the sawdust can be used in the barbecue for that world-renowned mesquite smoke flavor. Visit a local grocery store and you'll see people paying big bucks for mesquite wood chips packaged in five or 10-pound sacks. Make your own instead!

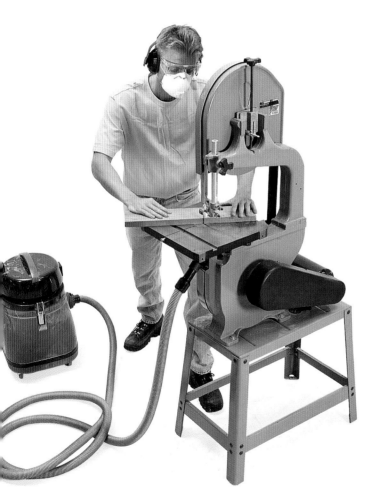

Mesquite dust can sometimes cause an allergic reaction, so wear a dust mask and use dust collection on your power tools.

by TIM JOHNSON

Birdseye Maple

Wild grain

YOU CAN TAME ITS UNRULY GRAIN

Birdseye maple is captivating, but has a reputation among woodworkers of being hard to find and miserable to work with. These are myths. Actually, birdseye is readily available in staggering varieties. I'll tell you where to find it and how to choose the best boards. And surprisingly, birdseye is easy to work with. I'll show you how to tame its unruly grain. And to top it off, I'll give you a recipe for a great-looking finish.

The Truth About Birdseye

"Birdseye" describes a figure pattern that occurs in the sugar maple tree (Acer saccharum). It's also found occasionally in several other varieties of wood. Individual birdseyes are randomly located pockets of irregular growth. Nobody knows what causes a tree to produce them, despite decades of research. We do know they have nothing to do with birds!

Birdseye's occurrence in sugar maple is not rare. In fact, a recent field study of old growth stands in the upper Midwest suggests that, because it occurs so frequently in old growth, birdseye could be considered the normal growth pattern for sugar maple. However, it typically occurs in such small amounts that its presence is considered a defect that actually reduces a tree's value. What's rare are trees with enough birdseye to make them commercially desirable.

Birdseye figure is caused by craters of wild grain that recur in successive layers of growth. On the face of a board you see the "birdseyes," on the end grain you see cone-shaped cylinders.

Annual rings

Cone-shaped cylinders

ART DIRECTION: PATRICK HELF • PHOTOGRAPHY: BILL ZUEHLKE

Tips for Buying Birdseye

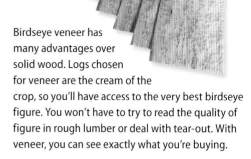

- **Buy surfaced material.** It's hard to pick good birdseye from rough lumber, which is the way you're most likely to find it. Even if you're accustomed to looking at rough-sawn material, it'll be tough to see the figure. Sometimes it's even hard to differentiate between light-colored sapwood and dark-colored heartwood. It's easier to choose from birdseye that's been planed "hit-and-miss." This light planing sacrifices a bit of the board's working thickness so you can see what you're buying, but the trade-off is worthwhile.

- **Look for flat boards.** Birdseye's ornery grain gives it a tendency to warp or cup as it dries. If you can't find boards that are flat, look for ones that are extra thick so you can plane them flat and still end up with the thickness you want. You may need to buy thicker stock (5/4 instead of 4/4, for example).

Birdseye veneer has many advantages over solid wood. Logs chosen for veneer are the cream of the crop, so you'll have access to the very best birdseye figure. You won't have to try to read the quality of figure in rough lumber or deal with tear-out. With veneer, you can see exactly what you're buying.

- **Order from a specialist.** Few lumberyards stock birdseye. The only way to get it may be through a mail-order supplier. There are several that specialize in figured woods. These suppliers have experience, knowledge, and inventory.

- **Consider using birdseye veneer,** especially for large surfaces like tabletops and cabinet sides. The color and figure varies so much in solid birdseye lumber that it's hard to find boards that look good together. Sheets of birdseye veneer have a consistent appearance because they're sawn sequentially from the same log. You'll save money, too. "AAA" grade veneer costs about $6.50 a square foot, compared to $8 per bd. ft. of "AAA" 4/4 rough stock, and it's much cheaper to ship.

Learn About Grading

Specialty suppliers see more birdseye in a day than most of us see in a lifetime. Take advantage of their experience. They grade their inventory board by board, according to several factors. When talking to them, it's helpful to know the criteria they use:

DESK BY JOEL SIMON, BLOOMINGTON, MN

"A"
"Light"

"AA"
"Medium"
"Good"

"AAA"
"Heavy"
"Strong"

- Figure quality is determined by the density of the birdseyes and the consistency of their pattern across the board.
- Consistent light color is desirable, as it is with regular maple.
- Wide boards and long boards cost more.

A long, wide board graded "AAA, sapwood both faces" will cost a pretty penny—up to $10 a bd. ft., and you'll have to factor in the cost of shipping. For the strong of heart, some suppliers list even higher grades—up to "AAAAA" or "museum quality." Instrument makers often seek pieces in these superior grades. Usually, your wallet helps you choose which grade to buy.

The more densely packed the birdseye, the higher the grade. There are no industry standards, so the grading is somewhat subjective. Some suppliers use letter grades, others use words.

All heart

Heart and sap

All sap

Boards that are light-colored on both sides are graded highest. In maple, this is the sapwood. The presence of dark-colored heartwood degrades the board, even though the birdseye figure may be spectacular.

Plane Birdseye Without Tear-Out

Planing rough-sawn birdseye is a challenge because the eyes are pockets of swirling grain scattered all over the surface. When you run it through a planer, the birdseye figure tears out dramatically—usually with disastrous results. The commonly recommended alternative is to take the rough lumber to someone who has a drum sander for surfacing. Technical schools and cabinet shops often rent time on their machines, but you have to pay a minimum of $25 per hour. And it's a hassle.

Here's a much easier solution. Wet the surface before you joint or plane it. Don't worry about warping. Planing removes the wet layer before the moisture affects the board.

The effect of wet-planing on your machines will be negligible if you follow these simple maintenance procedures. Be sure to unplug the jointer or planer before performing any maintenance.

- Moisture causes rust. Keep cast iron tables and fences protected with paste wax or a metal sealer.
- Use a dust collector to draw the wet shavings away from the machine—they contain all the moisture.
- After you've finished running the birdseye, wipe the cast iron tables dry with an absorbent cloth. Then run a dry board through the machine. The friction-generated heat helps evaporate any remaining moisture.
- Wipe the pressure roller, cutterhead, knives and other effected surfaces with denatured alcohol. Don't cut yourself on the knives.

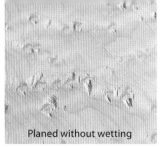

Planed without wetting

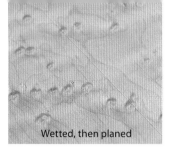

Wetted, then planed

Tear-out is typical when you run a birdseye board through a planer. The grain changes direction around each birdseye, so it doesn't matter which way you run the board. It's gonna tear out in chunks.

Tear-out is dramatically reduced when a birdseye board is wetted just before planing. (Look at the birdseye pattern—this is the same board as the one on the left!)

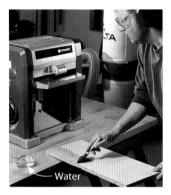

Water

Get birdseye boards wet before you plane them. Let the water soak in for a couple seconds before you run it through the planer. Make shallow passes, removing only 1/32 in. at a time.

#80-Style scraper

Remove minor tear-out with a scraper or by sanding. Scraping is best because it's fast, quiet, and dust-free. Sanding is effective, but tedious. Hand planing birdseye's swirling grain is likely to cause as much tear-out as it removes.

Penetrating oil

A thin coat of penetrating oil (one part oil, two parts mineral spirits) followed by a seal coat of shellac and topped with varnish is a great finish for birdseye. It warms the color, brings out the figure and protects the surface.

Sand or Scrape

After wet-planing you have to remove mill marks and minor tear-out before the birdseye is ready for finishing. It's too risky to try doing this with a hand plane—even one that's finely tuned. One bad pass can ruin everything. It's safer to sand or scrape.

A random-orbit sander helps make sanding less tedious, but sanding dust lodges in torn-out areas, making it hard to know when to quit. A scraper is better. It makes shavings instead of dust, so you can see when the tear-out is gone. Use the random-orbit sander for final smoothing, after scraping.

Easy Finishing

Even the simplest wipe-on finish makes birdseye look good. Here's how to make it look great:

- A coat of penetrating oil, like tung or linseed, brings out the birdseyes and adds a warm amber tone.
- A thin coat of dewaxed shellac on top of the oil makes the figure shimmer.
- For non-wear surfaces, buffing the shellac with wax adds luster. Protect tabletops and other wear surfaces by topcoating with lacquer or varnish. These finishes adhere to dewaxed shellac that's been lightly sanded.
- To minimize yellowing skip the oil. Start with a seal coat of dewaxed super-blond shellac and top it with waterborne polyurethane. Waterborne finishes are clear and don't yellow with age.
- If you want to color birdseye, don't use traditional wood stains—use transparent dyes instead.

by TOM CASPAR

Mahogany and Its Look-Alikes

ARE LESS-EXPENSIVE AFRICAN AND PHILIPPINE "MAHOGANY" JUST AS GOOD?

Stunning grain. Huge boards. Highly rot resistant. A dream (or a nightmare) to work. What one wood fits this bill? Mahogany, of course.

Even the plainest mahogany boards are quite beautiful, because the color is usually a deep, rich coppery red. Mahogany trees are huge, towering up to 150 ft. over the rain forest floor, and are often sawed into very wide boards up to 4-in. thick. The bombé chest, above right, was made from one 24-in.-wide board, 3-in. thick and 16-ft. long!

With all these good qualities, why aren't we all lining up at the lumberyard for mahogany boards? Because it's expensive, about $5 to $9 per bd. ft. It's so expensive that exporters of other woods have worked "mahogany" into the street names of their products and succeeded in confusing the heck out of woodworkers. Let's clear the air a bit and compare these species side by side.

American Mahogany

This is the real McCoy. American mahogany comes from Central and South America, and has been prized for fine furniture and boat building since the eighteenth century.

There are actually two different kinds of American mahogany: Cuban or Santo Domingo mahogany (Swietenia mahogani) and Honduras mahogany (Swietenia macrophylla). It was the denser, darker Cuban variety that first

American mahogany is one of the world's most beautiful woods. Its price has been rising slowly but steadily as these South American trees become more expensive to fell, process and export. No wonder everybody's looking for substitutes!

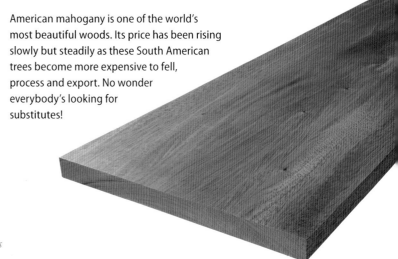

Fig. A Guide to Mahogany

Common Name	Also Known As	Species	Cost/bd.ft.
American mahogany	Honduras mahogany	Swietenia macrophylla	$5-9
African mahogany	Khaya	Khaya ivorensis	$4-8
African mahogany	Sapele	Entandrophragma cylindricum	$5-10
Philippine mahogany	Lauan	various species of Shorea	$3-4

American mahogany has long been favored for its outstanding working qualities, especially with hand tools. It's easy to clearly mark with a knife or pencil, smooth with a hand plane and pare with a chisel. Dense boards are usually better for handwork than lightweight boards.

excited furniture makers 300 years ago, but there's very little of it left today. When selling mahogany, most lumber dealers are referring to the Honduras type.

Honduras mahogany primarily comes from South America. The best and densest grades, those most like the legendary Cuban mahogany, are exported from the rain forests of Peru. Honduras mahogany is still readily available, but it's been logged very heavily, often at the expense of a healthy forest. There's been quite an international effort to certify more responsible logging practices. For more on certified and plantation-grown mahogany, go to *www.certifiedwood.org.*

Quartersawn Mahogany is Harder to Work

Many mahogany trees have an unusual internal structure called "interlocked grain." When boards are plainsawn (with the growth rings more or less parallel to the wide face), interlocked grain makes beautiful swirling patterns. When boards are quartersawn (with the growth rings at right angles to the wide face), interlocked grain makes a ribbon-stripe figure.

Plainsawn mahogany is generally a pleasure to work, but quartersawn mahogany can be a bear. Each ribbon in a quartersawn board indicates a change in grain or fiber direction. When planing or jointing, you can't win. Whatever direction you feed a quartersawn board, you may get nasty tear-out.

Common mahogany look-alikes include Khaya, Sapele, and Lauan. (They're pronounced Kigh-yah, Sah-pee-lee and Loo-ahn.) Khaya and Sapele are often called African mahogany and are in the same botanical family, Meliaceae, as American mahogany. Lauan is sold as Philippine mahogany, but it's not in the same botanical family.

Khaya

Sapele

Lauan

ART DIRECTION: VERN JOHNSON • PHOTOGRAPHY: MIKE HABERMANN, UNLESS OTHERWISE INDICATED • ILLUSTRATION: FRANK ROHRBACH • RESEARCH ASSISTANT: KAREN NAKAMURA

Plainsawn   **Quartersawn**

American Mahogany

Sapele

Khaya

Quartersawn boards often have a ribbon-striped appearance, caused by the grain or fibers periodically changing direction. This means that quartersawn boards often have tear-out problems. American mahogany is generally plainsawn, but Khaya and Sapele are usually quartersawn to show off their strong ribbon-stripe figure.

Color, Density, and Figure Are All Over the Map

Looking over a pile of roughsawn American mahogany, you might think all the boards are pretty much the same. Pick up a few, however, and you notice that some are a lot heavier than others. Plane their surfaces, and you'll see an astonishingly wide range of color.

Few woods are as variable in density, color, and figure as American mahogany. In addition to their lower cost, that's why so many other woods can be marketed as "mahogany," or blended with American mahogany as showy veneers or secondary solid woods (right).

Steer away from the least dense boards. Often they have the blandest color, but more importantly, the wood is softer and doesn't surface well. You'll get patches of fuzzy grain that are difficult to smooth (bottom, page 147).

Mahoganies from Africa: Khaya and Sapele

Khaya and Sapele have long been used as fine furniture woods, particularly in Europe. Both are less durable for outdoor furniture than American mahogany.

Pommele Sapele, $5

Fiddleback Makore, $3.50

Mottled Makore, heavy figure, $2.75

Quartersawn Sapele, $1.10

Quilted Makore, $3.50

Seagrass and Fiddleback American Mahogany, $1.50

Crotch Khaya, $4 to $8

Quartersawn Khaya, $1.10

Mottled Makore, low-medium figure, $1.45

Seagrass American Mahogany, $1.50

A wide range of figure and color is available in American mahogany and other closely related veneers. Few other woods have so many different faces. With careful staining, all these veneers can be blended with solid American mahogany, Khaya or Sapele. Color and pattern "trade names" vary with different suppliers. To buy the veneers shown above, see Sources, page 204. Prices are given per square foot. These pieces are 9-in. wide.

Khaya and Sapele are available from many lumber dealers. See Sources, page 204, for a dealer who'll ship through the mail.

Khaya is a gorgeous wood, and a good substitute for American mahogany. In fact, with many boards, it's darned hard to tell the two woods apart. Khaya is generally quartersawn to produce a distinctive ribbony appearance.

BILL RAY

Outdoor furniture made of American mahogany will last many years because it's naturally rot resistant. Like all woods, it slowly turns a silvery gray color outdoors unless it's stained or varnished. Khaya and Sapele are also good choices for outdoor projects, but won't last as long.

Fig. B Rot Resistance

Type	Degree of Rot Resistance
Teak	Durable
White Oak	Durable
American mahogany	Durable
Khaya	Moderately durable
Sapele	Moderately durable
Dark red Lauan	Moderately durable
Light red Lauan	Not durable

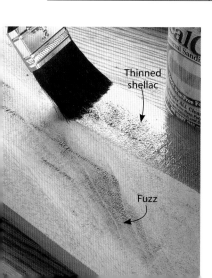

Thinned shellac

Fuzz

Fuzzy grain is an annoying problem with all of the mahogany-related woods, especially in less-dense boards. Every once in a while you'll come across a lightweight board that you just can't get smooth, even with power sanding. Before giving up, try stiffening the fibers with a wash coat of shellac, and then sanding.

Khaya works well, but it's not on par with the best grades of American mahogany. It's more prone to tear-out, and there's a greater chance you'll get some boards with fuzzy surface patches that are very hard to smooth (bottom). Khaya is generally softer, too, and won't hold as crisp an edge as American mahogany. That means it's not as good for fine detail in moldings and carvings.

Sapele has a finer texture than American mahogany. It's easier to tell the two apart, but Sapele is still a good substitute. Like Khaya, Sapele is often quartersawn to reveal a ribbon-stripe grain pattern, but its ribbons are often narrower and closer together. With tighter interlocked grain, Sapele is also prone to tear-out.

Philippine Mahogany: Lauan

Lauan is inexpensive, plentiful and widely used in plywood, trim moldings and commercial furniture. But it's not a true mahogany. Lauan is one of many woods that are loosely called "Philippine mahogany." They all come from the Far East, are generally identified by their color, and have varied properties. The redder varieties are heavier and much more rot resistant than the lighter varieties, for example.

Most of the Lauan sold in the U.S. as lumber and plywood is pretty consistent. It's a softer and lighter wood than American mahogany, dents easily with your fingernail and has a tendency to splinter. It has little of the beautiful figure of American mahogany and a much coarser texture. For the most part, you shouldn't use it as the show wood on a piece of fine furniture.

Special Finishes

Finishing wood is a craft and an art, and achieving the results you want often depend on the finish more than on any other factor. With the right finish materials and finishing techniques, you'll be able to bring out the best in the wood you have, and you'll even be able to make one wood species look like another. The stories in this section show you how to:

- stain and finish ordinary pine so it looks like a million bucks;
- fill the pores of open-grained woods so they'll take a glassy polish;
- bleach dark wood lighter and stain light wood darker, two skills that come together in managing the sapwood on cherry and walnut boards;
- achieve the precise look you want on ordinary oak, everybody's favorite domestic hardwood.

❮ **Finishing Touch**—*The wood-finisher's skill really comes to the forefront in furniture repair; you've got to make the new part, such as this turned leg, match the old wood on the rest of the table (background). In the case of highly colored woods like walnut, the best answer may be to bleach the color out of new wood, then stain it to match the old.*

by TIM JOHNSON

Staining Pine

MAKE THIS INEXPENSIVE WOOD LOOK LIKE A MILLION BUCKS

Antique pine often has a dark, mellow color. Unfortunately, when woodworkers try to duplicate that color on new pine by using stain, the results are usually disappointing. It's easy to end up with mega-blotches and it's hard to avoid "grain reversal," a peculiar effect that makes stained pine look unnatural (photo below). It doesn't have to be that way, though. If you follow the process presented here, you can give pine deep, rich-looking color without losing it's natural appearance.

Pine is hard to stain for a couple of reasons. First, its grain is unevenly dense. Typical wood stains cause grain reversal because they color only the porous earlywood; they can't penetrate the dense latewood. Second, pine's surface is usually loaded with randomly occurring figure and super-absorbent pockets that suck up stain and look blotchy.

Our staining process includes four ingredients, water-based wood conditioner, water-soluble wood dye, dewaxed shellac and oil-based glaze (see Sources, page 204). Our process isn't fast, because there are several steps. But it isn't hard, and it's home-shop friendly. You don't need any special finishing equipment, just brushes and rags.

In a nutshell, the conditioner partially seals the wood's surface to control blotching. Dyes penetrate both the earlywood and latewood, so they minimize grain reversal. Shellac and glaze add color in layers, creating depth and richness. This coloring process works on all types of pine, although the end result varies from one species to another.

Staining usually causes blotches and always makes pine's porous earlywood darker than its dense latewood, just the opposite of unstained pine (inset). This transformation is called "grain reversal."

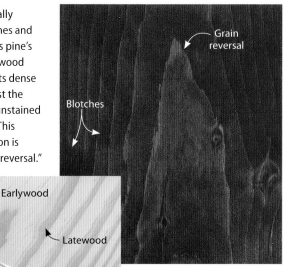

Grain reversal

Blotches

Earlywood

Latewood

Before You Stain

Fill gaps and stabilize loose knots with epoxy. Tape the back of the knot so the epoxy can't leak out.

Sand with a block angled across the growth rings. Because of the difference in hardness between the earlywood and latewood, bridging as many rings as possible helps to keep the surface level.

Preemptive grain-raising is a must-do for all water-based finishes. After you've finished sanding, dampen the surface, to raise the grain. Then sand it again, with 400-grit sandpaper.

Look Before You Leap

Before you touch your project with a brush or rag, get familiar with the materials and the process by practicing on good-sized pieces of scrap. Experiment on end grain, face grain, and veneered stock. Practice until you're comfortable with the process and know what to expect.

Fix Loose Knots

Before you sand, stabilize any loose knots by dribbling epoxy into the gaps (photo A). To make cleanup easier, keep it off the surrounding wood surfaces. After the epoxy has set, sand it flush with the surface. Clear epoxy transmits the dark color of the knot. If your epoxy cures milky-white, touch it up later, after you've dyed the wood and sealed it with shellac.

Sand Thoroughly

A good-looking finish always starts with a thorough sanding job, especially with a soft wood like pine. Here are some guidelines:

Sand with a block. Orbital sanders leave swirl marks that make the stained surface look muddy. After power sanding, always sand by hand, using a block, before you go on to the next grit (Photo B). Sanding with finger pressure alone wears away the soft earlywood, creating an uneven surface.

Change paper often. Pine gums up ordinary sandpaper with pitch-laden dust that quickly renders it useless. Dull paper mashes the wood fibers instead of cutting them, which also creates a muddy appearance when you stain. Stearated sandpaper lasts longer (see Sources, page 204).

Brush on two generous coats of water-based conditioner. With each application, keep the surface wet for three to five minutes, then wipe off the excess. Let the conditioner dry thoroughly, then sand it with 400-grit paper. Go lightly on contours and edges, so you don't cut through.

Dissolve powdered dye in hot water. When the powder is completely dissolved, transfer it to a lidded container and let it cool.

Brush on a liberal coat of dye and keep the surface wet. Wipe the end grain occasionally to check its appearance. After the surface is uniformly colored, wipe off the excess dye and let the wood dry. Then repeat the process.

Sand up to 220 grit. First, level the surface with 100-grit paper. Then work through the grits to create finer and finer scratch patterns. 220-grit scratches are fine enough to disappear when you stain, as long as they don't go across the grain.

Raise the Grain

Sanding leaves some fibers bent over. Water-based finishes swell these fibers so they stand up, leaving a rough surface. For smooth results with these finishes, raise the grain prior to finishing. (Photo C).

Two Coats of Conditioner

Water-based wood conditioner makes water-based dye easy to apply. It limits the dye's penetration by partially sealing the wood. Two coats are necessary to control blotching (Step 1).

Keep the surface wet until you wipe it, then wipe thoroughly. Conditioner allowed to dry on the surface will seal so well the dye won't penetrate.

Two Coats of Dye

We used "antique cherry brown" water-soluble dye powder. Dissolve the dye at the label-recommended ratio of 1-oz. powder to 2-qts. hot water (Step 2). Cool the solution to room temperature before use.

On the conditioned surface, the dye acts like a liquid oil stain (Step 3). Let it penetrate for a couple minutes before wiping. The second coat of dye imparts a deeper more uniform color.

It's tough to get uniform penetration on end grain. Fortunately, you can minimize any uneven appearance later with the colored glaze.

When you have a large surface to cover, use a spray bottle to apply the dye and a brush to spread it. Simply re-spray previously worked areas to keep the entire surface wet until you're ready to wipe it dry. Spraying and brushing also works great on vertical surfaces. Start at the bottom and work your way up.

Two Coats of Shellac

Shellac prepares the dyed surface for glazing. It also keeps pitch sealed in the wood. Without shellac, pine's pitch can bleed into oil-based finishes, leaving fissures or shiny spots that remain tacky, especially around knots.

Apply Glaze

Glaze is nothing more than paint formulated for wiping. It's easy to make your own pro-quality glaze (Step 5). Artist's oils contain high-quality pigments for pure, clear color. Glaze medium makes the artist's oil easy to spread and quick to dry (within 24 hours).

Glazing adds a second, separate layer of color that really makes the pine come alive (Step 6).

Topcoats

You need to protect this layered finish with clear topcoats. Any topcoat will work as long as you wait until the glaze has completely dried. To check, wipe the surface gently with a cotton rag. If it picks up any color, wait another day.

Brush on two generous coats of water-based conditioner. With each application, keep the surface wet for three to five minutes, then wipe off the excess. Let the conditioner dry thoroughly, then sand it with 400-grit paper. Go lightly on contours and edges, so you don't cut through.

Make your own glaze by dissolving artist's oil into glaze medium. You don't have to be scientific about the ratio as long as you use only one color. Don't go overboard with the amount you mix—a little glaze goes a long way.

Glaze acts as a toner on the sealed surface, resulting in a deep, rich color and a uniform appearance. Just brush it on and wipe it off. Blend uneven areas by varying the amount of glaze you leave on the surface.

by MICHAEL DRESDNER

Water-Borne Pore Fillers

THE FIRST STEP TO A GLASS-SMOOTH FINISH

Some of our favorite woods have large, open pores on the surface. Mahogany, walnut, teak, koa, ash, oak, and rosewood all fall into this category. With these and other woods you have a choice; apply a thin finish that lets the pores show, or use pore filler to create a glass-smooth, pore-free surface. Which you choose is strictly a matter of taste, but if you go for the second option, known as a "filled finish," you need to know about pore fillers.

What Is a Pore Filler?

Pore filler, also called semi-paste filler, is a thick mixture of inert solids and resin that can be packed into wood pores. The inert solids are usually ground-up sand, but they can be powdered rock (talc or pumice) or wood dust (called wood flour). The resin in the mix acts as a binder to keep the solids together and stuck in the wood pores.

In theory, you could fill the pores by building up layer after layer of finish and sanding it back. However, this is a very tedious process, and is likely to result in pores showing up again some months later as the finish packed into them shrinks. Pore filler is a quicker and more reliable path to the same end.

Filler does not shrink after it dries. As a result, once applied, it levels the entire surface of the wood, pores and all. Don't confuse pore filler with wood putty, which is a thicker mixture meant for filling gouges and dings in wood. Pore filler is too thin to fill large gouges, and putty is too thick to fill pores easily.

When to Use Them

On woods with very fine pores, such as maple, cherry, poplar, and most softwoods, filler isn't necessary. On large-pored wood, filler can be used for two main reasons: to create a level base for the finish, and to create color contrast.

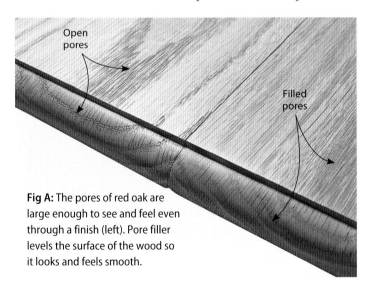

Open pores

Filled pores

Fig A: The pores of red oak are large enough to see and feel even through a finish (left). Pore filler levels the surface of the wood so it looks and feels smooth.

Gloss finishes and solid colors benefit greatly from a level finishing surface. When pores show under these finishes they tend to detract from the elegant appearance. Even worse, when you try to polish a high-gloss finish with open pores, the rubbing compound will often pack into them, leaving you with an unsightly mess. When you finish open-pored woods with either a solid color or with a gloss finish, use pore filler first.

A colored pore filler can either change the overall color of the wood or create an interesting contrast between the wood and its pores. A pore filler that is darker than the general color of the wood creates contrast between the pores and the background wood. This makes the wood appear darker and adds richness and character to the wood by making the pores more obvious (Photo 7). The same is true of a light pore filler. It creates contrast while making the wood lighter in color. And while wood purists may blanch, using pore filler colored to contrast with typical wood tones can create stunning effects that Mother Nature never imagined (Photo 6).

Oil vs. Water

Pore fillers are sold both in oil-based and water-borne varieties. They both do the same basic job, but water-borne fillers have several advantages. They have fewer annoying fumes, dry faster, and are compatible with virtually any finish: water-borne, oil-based, shellac, or lacquer.

Water-borne pore filler is available in a wide range of typical wood colors or neutral (a pale ecru color). If you find it necessary, you can alter the colors yourself using UTCs

Work filler into the pores by rubbing with a white nylon pad. White pads are the finest of the nylon abrasives, containing only talc. If the filler sets up too fast, spray it with water to keep it workable.

Squeegee the excess filler slurry from the surface, while it's still wet. A credit card makes a great squeegee. Let the filler dry completely before sanding.

Clean a profiled edge using a credit card cut to match the profile. Curved surfaces and inside corners are the toughest areas to clean of excess filler. Credit cards can be cut and filed so they can get into tight areas.

Sand with 220-grit, self-lubricating sandpaper to remove the dried filler from the surface. This is an important step. Any filler left on the surface shows up when the piece is finished, so be thorough.

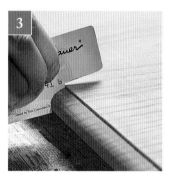

Wipe the surface clean with a cloth dampened with water (about as damp as a healthy dog's nose) to remove the last bit of sanding dust and it's ready to finish.

(universal tinting colors), which come as thick liquids or pastes. UTCs can usually be found at a well-stocked paint or home store, or at woodworking specialty stores. UTCs usually slow down the filler's drying time.

Applying Water-Borne Filler

Instead of brushing, I scrub water-borne fillers directly into the wood using the finest nylon abrasive pads—the white ones. Gray pads are the second finest. The pad lets me get the filler onto the wood and pack it into the pores all in one step.

As soon as I get it scrubbed in, I squeegee off all of the excess with a plastic scraper or old credit card. Once the excess is squeegeed off, I let the filler dry. In a few hours, depending on the humidity, I can go back, sand the surface, clean off the sanding dust with a cloth dampened lightly with water, and the piece is ready for finish.

New: Clear Water-Borne Fillers

These new fillers offer the option of filling pores without adding any color whatsoever. For some woods, like figured koa and walnut (photo 8), the incredible beauty of the wood is only dulled by stain, even when it is only in the pores. For such woods, the new fillers are a delight.

Of the two I have used, one looks and feels more like a mousse or an airy wax, while the other is a runny paste. Both are easy to use and dry quite fast, often in under an hour, depending on humidity. Apply them the same way as other water-borne fillers. The one drawback is that they shrink quite a bit during drying, so for effective filling, you need to make several applications.

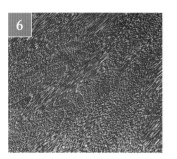

6 An eye-catching look can be achieved by using a colored filler that contrasts with the natural tones of the wood (above, top) or by applying contrasting-colored pore filler over a colored, sealed surface (left). Use 320-grit sandpaper to remove the filler without disturbing the color below.

7 Dark-colored filler makes the sample on the right appear darker than its companion, which has neutral filler. Both samples came from the same mahogany board.

8 A clear filler on walnut allows a glass-smooth surface without affecting the natural range of color in the wood.

by MICHAEL DRESDNER

Bleaching Wood

SUBTRACT COLOR TO ADD LIFE

There are four types of bleach that woodworkers commonly use: chlorine, two-part wood bleach, oxalic acid, and peroxide. Two-part bleach changes the actual color of wood and the other three remove stains. Read on to find out what each one does and how to use them safely.

Chlorine Bleach

Common household laundry bleach (sodium hypochlorite) will kill mildew on your deck and outdoor furniture, and will remove dye-based stain, but not pigment-based stain, from wood. Chlorine bleach can irritate skin and mucous membranes, so wear gloves and goggles.

Deck cleaner. To remove mildew from your deck or exterior furniture, first hose off the wood to remove any loose debris. Mix about a quart of chlorine bleach (Clorox, Purex, etc.) to each gallon of water. Use a synthetic-bristle brush and scrub the surface with the bleach mixture. Be sure to wear goggles—it's easy to splash. Reapply the bleach if necessary in order to keep the surface wet for about 15 minutes. Then, brush off the surface again and hose it down thoroughly with water. Keep the runoff away from plants, pets, and other wildlife.

Fortunately, deck stains are formulated with pigments, so they are not affected by the bleach. Let the wood dry completely if you plan to re-stain. If you live in an area where mildew is a problem, choose a deck stain that contains a mildewcide, or add some yourself. Most home centers and paint stores sell them.

Dye remover. Chlorine bleach will remove most dye-based stains from raw wood but will not lighten the wood itself. This is handy to know if you finish your project with a dye, and then decide you want to "erase" it and start over. Chlorine bleach will also remove old dye that you might encounter during a refinishing project.

Alabaster Oak Wardrobe: Use bleach like stain. Two-part wood bleach turns red oak bone-white, without obscuring the grain the way a pickling stain would. The top coat is water-based polyurethane.

WARDROBE BY TIM JOHNSON, MINNEAPOLIS, MINN., 1991
PHOTO: MIKE KEEFE

Dye-Based Stain   Raw Wood   Pigment-Based Stain

Chlorine bleach, full strength, easily removes most dye-based stain (left) but will not bleach raw wood white (center), nor will it remove pigment-based stain (right).

Use a synthetic-bristle brush or a clean rag to apply the bleach full strength. It should remove the color by the time it dries, but for stubborn stains, repeat the process. If you are removing the stain from an old piece of furniture that you are refinishing, make sure all the finish is off the surface and lightly scuff-sand it first. Bleach will not go through a finish.

As bleach dries, it breaks down to salt and water. Once the water evaporates, you'll have salt residue on the wood. Brush it off before you finish the wood.

Two-Part (A/B) Wood Bleach

Wood bleach actually lightens the color of wood. It can also de-color many pigments and dyes.

A package of wood bleach contains two bottles, usually labeled "A" and "B." One contains lye (sodium hydroxide) and the other peroxide (hydrogen peroxide). The bleaching action occurs when the two chemicals come together in contact with wood.

Instructions for use vary from brand to brand. Some say to put part A on

Two-part wood bleach takes the color out of most dark woods and blends maple heartwood color with its sapwood.

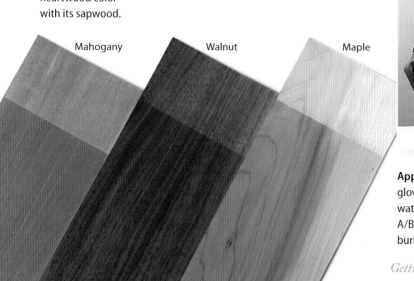

Mahogany   Walnut   Maple

Apply A/B bleach safely. Wear long neoprene gloves, with ends cuffed to catch drips, a waterproof apron, and goggles. Brush carefully. A/B bleach is extremely caustic and will quickly burn your skin and eyes.

first, then apply B before A dries. Others suggest mixing the two just before application. The object is to get both chemicals and the wood all in the same place at the same time. Read the directions.

Use a synthetic-bristle brush or a clean rag to apply the bleach. When the lye goes on first, it initially darkens the wood. Once the peroxide goes on, it is likely to foam as it reacts with the wood and lye. Let the wood dry completely, usually overnight, then sponge off all residue with plenty of clean water.

Oxalic Acid

Iron, in the form of nails, hardware, or even bits of steel wool, often leaves a blackish stain on woods high in tannin, like oak. A wash of oxalic solution removes these stains as well as the grayed color of oxidized wood.

Oxalic acid is sold in most hardware stores and home centers as a dry, white crystalline powder. The crystals are toxic and irritating to mucous membranes, so wear goggles and a dust mask when handling the dry powder. In a glass or plastic container, dissolve an ounce of oxalic acid into a pint of warm water.

Make certain that you have removed all the offending metal before you bleach the wood. Sometimes stains are caused by broken-off nails or bits of fencing that are hidden in the wood. Wet the surface with the oxalic acid mixture and let it dry. Repeat if the stain is not completely gone. Once dry, sponge the wood with plenty

of clean water to remove the crystalline residue. Any oxalic acid residue left in the wood will make irritating dust when you sand, so wear a dust mask and eye protection.

Peroxide

Maple is prone to a particular type of blue stain that is caused by mold during the drying process. A strong, 35-percent peroxide solution, like the "B" portion of wood bleach, can usually remove the stain.

Concentrated peroxide is very caustic, so wear goggles, gloves, and a waterproof apron.

You can buy 35-percent peroxide solution from a chemical supply company, or borrow it from your box of two-part wood bleach. Flood it onto the maple with a foam brush and let it dry completely. There is no need to wash it down, since peroxide (H_2O_2) neutralizes itself to water and oxygen. In extreme cases, when the peroxide alone won't do the trick, two-part wood bleach will.

Oxalic acid: Dissolved in water, removes black iron stains like magic from tannin-rich wood like oak.

by JEFF GORTON

Tips for Finishing Walnut

USE DYES AND BLEACH TO MATCH COLOR

There's no denying that most walnut looks great with nothing more than a few coats of oil. Here we'll show you some tricks to make your walnut projects look even better.

Make Sapwood Disappear

Even select walnut boards are likely to contain an occasional streak of light-colored sapwood. If you can't afford the luxury of avoiding all sapwood, we'll show you how to make it less conspicuous. Even though the initial investment for dye, shellac and glaze materials will set you back about $100, most of these products are highly concentrated and should last you many years.

Dyeing sapwood looks paint-by-number simple but there are a few tricks. The key to the process is getting the dye color to match the heartwood color. Don't bother with dyes labeled "walnut." Buy red, blue, yellow and black water-soluble dye powder and custom mix a sapwood dye according to the recipe on p. 162. We gradually adjusted the color of the dye by adding drops of blue and black to reach the purplish gray hue of kiln-dried walnut. An eye-dropper works great for this. Air-dried walnut has more red.

Adjust your dye accordingly using the Color Mixing Chart on p. 162 as a guide.

We're using water-soluble dye because it resists fading in sunlight better than alcohol-soluble dye and is easy to apply without leaving lap marks. One drawback, however, is its tendency to raise wood grain. Minimize grain raising by wetting the wood, letting it dry, and sanding off the raised grain with 220-grit sandpaper before applying the dye. Don't sand too much or you'll expose new wood and negate the effect.

Here are a few more tips for working with water-soluble dye:

- Wet the end grain before dyeing it to keep it from soaking up too much dye.
- Start with a diluted dye; you can always increase the intensity of the color by adding a "layer" of more concentrated dye.
- Adjust the color by adding another layer. Wipe on green dye to decrease red, for example.
- The color you see when you apply the dye to the wood is close to the color you'll end up with. The wood will look dull when the dye dries, but the "wet" color will return when the finish is applied.

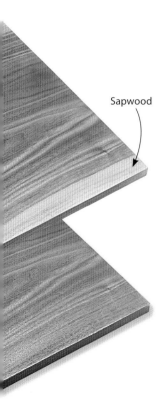

Sapwood

Color Mixing Chart

Red + Blue = Violet

Red + Yellow = Orange

Blue + Yellow = Green

Red + Yellow + Blue = Brown

To decrease Red add Green

To decrease Orange add Blue

To decrease Yellow add Violet

To darken a color add Black

Use a small artist's paint brush to carefully dye the sapwood, following along the grain line. Blend the edge of the dye into the heartwood with the corner of a damp rag. Dampen the wood before applying the dye.

Apply the glaze with a rag or brush. Remove the excess, leaving a thin layer. Then use a good-quality paint brush with soft bristles to manipulate the glaze, to blend the dyed sapwood into the heartwood.

■ Lighten dyed wood by wiping off some dye with a damp rag. If you really goof, use household chlorine bleach to remove almost all of the dye.

Allow the dyed wood to dry overnight. Then seal the entire surface with a thin coat of brushed on shellac (about a 2-lb. cut of super-blonde). Allow sealer to dry and sand lightly with 320-grit sandpaper. If you're happy with the way the sapwood blends after sealer is applied, apply the final coats of finish. To blend the dyed sapwood more completely, and add greater depth and richer color, apply a thin layer of glaze before applying the final coats of finish.

Glaze is essentially thinned paint that's layered over a sealed surface. Commercially prepared glazes are available, or you can make your own. Mix up an oil glaze by combining artist's oil paint (available at art supply stores) with a glazing medium consisting of three parts boiled linseed oil, two parts mineral spirits and one part Japan drier, to the consistency of heavy cream. Pick up the following colors as a starter set for blending your own custom colors; burnt umber, raw umber, burnt sienna, raw sienna, Vandyke brown, yellow ochre, black and blue.

Complete the process of blending the sapwood by applying a layer of glaze, as shown in Photo 2. Keep the brush "dry" by removing excess glaze from the bristles with a rag. To add glaze in one section, "stipple" it on with the tips of the bristles and then smooth it. If you make a mistake, remove the glaze using a rag dampened with mineral spirits.

Allow the glaze to dry completely, a minimum of 24 hours, before applying the final coats of finish.

Sapwood Dye Recipe

Start by mixing each of the powdered dyes with hot distilled water or rainwater in its own glass or plastic container according to the instructions on the label. Then combine the liquid dyes in the proportions listed below to create the sapwood dye color.

1 part red   1 part blue

2 parts yellow   1½ parts black

Transfer a small amount of this dye to another container and dilute with up to 4 parts water. Check the intensity and hue on a scrap of walnut sapwood.

Matching Old Walnut

As walnut ages its color changes. Matching the cool, charcoal-gray color of new kiln-dried walnut to the mellow mahogany red or amber gold of aged walnut is a challenge faced by anyone who repairs old furniture.

In most cases the new walnut will have to be lightened before adding color with dye. Use two-part wood bleach, available at most hardware and paint stores. This bleach will lighten the walnut without removing all of the reddish tones. Mix and apply the bleach according to the instructions on the containers. Allow it to dry. Then lightly sand the surface with 220-grit sandpaper.

Aged walnut recipe

1 part red
2 parts yellow
½ part black

Once the wood has been lightened with bleach, mix dye to match the lightest, most prevalent color of the wood. If you're matching reddish walnut like ours, use our aged walnut recipe (above) to mix the dye and then adjust the color to match your project. The process of dyeing and glazing is the same as that for blending sapwood. We left extra glaze in the recesses around the turnings to duplicate the aged finish on the other legs.

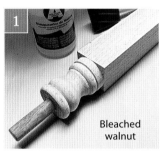

Bleached walnut

Bleach your replacement part by mixing two-part wood bleach according to the directions on the label and immediately applying it to the new walnut. Allow the bleach to dry and lightly sand the surface.

Dyed walnut

Dye the bleached wood to approximate the color of the aged walnut. Err on the light side. Allow the dye to dry. Then seal with a coat of 1-lb. cut shellac, allow to dry, and sand with 320-grit sandpaper.

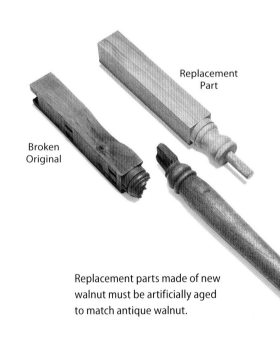

Replacement Part

Broken Original

Replacement parts made of new walnut must be artificially aged to match antique walnut.

Brush or wipe a thin layer of glaze over the dyed walnut. Remove the excess glaze with a rag or dry brush, leaving enough to match the color of the new piece to the aged walnut. Let the glaze dry before applying the final coats of finish.

Glazed walnut

Completed repair

Warming Up
Colorless Finishes

Water-borne varnishes and lacquer are often used on light-colored wood like maple to avoid the "yellowing" that occurs with traditional shellac and varnish finishes. Darker woods like walnut, on the other hand, look better with a "warmer" finish that brings out the rich, dark color.

If you plan on using a water-borne varnish or lacquer finish, consider warming up the walnut first with a coat of dye. We used the aged walnut recipe diluted three parts to one. Allow the dye to dry. Then brush on a sealer coat of a 2-lb. cut of dewaxed shellac to keep the water-borne finish from dissolving the dye. Dewaxed shellac makes an excellent undercoat for most water-borne and lacquer finishes, but check the label to be sure.

Dyed walnut with water-borne finish

Natural walnut with water-borne finish

Supplies
• 1 oz. bottles of yellow, red, blue and black water-soluble dye powder
• 1 lb. container super-blonde shellac flakes
• 1 qt. Behkol proprietary shellac solvent
• 1 oz. tube of burnt umber artist's oil
• 1 qt. mineral spirits
• 1 qt. boiled linseed oil
• 1 pt. Japan drier
• 2-part wood bleach
• 150-, 220-, 320-grit white aluminum-oxide non-loading sandpaper
• Tack cloths
• Small artist's brush
• 1½ in. disposable, pure-bristle brushes
• 1½ in. premium-quality natural-bristle brushes
• Lots of white cotton rags

Coloring Mismatched Walnut

The intensity and hue of walnut often varies from one board to another or between plywood veneer and solid lumber. These color differences can detract from the appearance of your finished project. Give your project a more cohesive look by dyeing the lighter wood and applying a glaze to even out the color differences. Use the same procedure we explained in "Make Sapwood Disappear," p. 161.

If you don't discover the mismatch until after you have applied a coat of oil or other finish, skip the dyeing step and blend the colors with glaze as we've done on the bookcase in these photos.

Walnut veneer with oil finish

Solid w. face fra

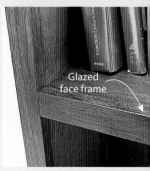

Glazed face frame

by TIM JOHNSON

Tips for Finishing Cherry

OIL IT, SPRAY IT, SHELLAC IT, OR GLAZE IT. THIS IS HOW TO MAKE CHERRY LOOK GREAT.

Cherry is gorgeous wood, but as you've probably discovered, it can be nasty to finish. Cherry boards come in all different colors, the sapwood and heartwood don't match, it can look really blotchy and it darkens as it ages.

Take advantage of my 28 years of experience with cherry. Here's everything I've learned about choosing lumber, getting rich color, a uniform appearance, and making a new cherry piece look 100 years old.

Color Varies from Board to Board

To make finishing easier, choose boards that look the same. Some suppliers sell boards from the same tree together, to ensure a good match. Usually, though, you'll be on your own.

If you plan to use solid cherry along with cherry plywood, stand the solid stock against the veneer in good, natural light, so you can compare the colors. Wetting the surfaces with mineral spirits is another way to get a true indication of color.

If you can't find enough boards of the same color for your entire project, group similar ones together for the various parts. Everyone will see that single off-colored board in the top, but no one will notice if one side of a cabinet is a slightly different.

Cherry Darkens Over Time

Cherry's color deepens from a pale pinkish-tan to a deep red-brown as a result of its exposure to air and light. The color change is so rapid at first that within hours, a partially covered board can develop a shadow line that can be hard to sand out. It's important to keep freshly planed boards either completely covered or completely exposed.

After the first couple of weeks, darkening becomes more gradual. Most finishes will slow cherry's color change, especially ones with UV blockers (check the label), but they don't stop it. At first, linseed and tung oil finishes give cherry a deeper, richer appearance than film-forming finishes like shellac, lacquer and polyurethane . But after a year or so, they'll all look pretty much the same.

If you want to give cherry a dark color right away, don't use oil stain. It colors cherry's pores and makes it look unnatural. Colored glazes or finishes using chemical reactions work best (page 172).

Sapwood and Heartwood

The difference between cherry's white sapwood and rosy-tan heartwood becomes more distinct over time. The heartwood darkens, but the sapwood doesn't. The best way to deal with sapwood is to cut it off, but it can be finished to blend with the heartwood (see Sidebar, page 169).

Thirsty Spots and Curly Figure

Most cherry boards contain extra-absorbent spots and pockets of curly figure that are more distracting than spectacular. With both "problems," finishing results in a mottled appearance. To some, this is part of cherry's inherent beauty; to others, it just looks blotchy. Before you choose a finish, check your boards for mottling by wiping them with mineral spirits.

Choosing a Finish

There are two types of finishes for sealing and protecting wood: Those that dry to a hard film and those that don't.

Film-forming finishes can be applied by wiping, brushing, or spraying. Each layer you apply builds the thickness of the film. Finishes made from drying oils soak into the wood's pores, but don't harden enough to form a surface film. They have to be wiped, because you can't leave any on the surface. On cherry, drying oil finishes emphasize a mottled appearance. Film-forming finishes, like shellac, lacquer and polyurethane, minimize it. Polyurethane disguises mottling and curly figure the best, but it gives cherry less depth than shellac or lacquer.

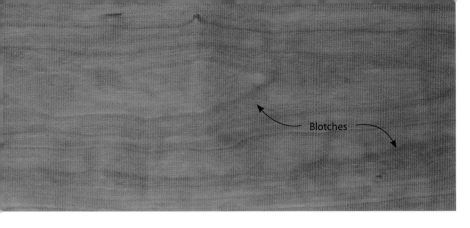

Blotches

Oil finish gives cherry a rich tone, because of its amber color, but the results are unpredictable. Cherry often absorbs oil unevenly, and parts that absorb a lot of oil look darker. The result is a mottled appearance. You'll either see this as part of cherry's appealing character or as unattractive blotches.

Wipe-On Drying Oil

Tung oil and boiled linseed oil soak into the wood, lodging in even the tiniest pores. This makes cherry's super-absorbent spots and curly figure stand out. The deep-amber color of these oils amplifies the effect. If you like mottled cherry, use a drying oil finish.

Wipe-ons are the most worry-free finishes to apply. They're dust-free and you don't have to contend with drips, sags, or brush marks. Wiping can be tedious work, though, and you'll have to safely dispose of oil-soaked rags.

Brush, pour or rub the oil on the wood, according the manufacturer's directions. These finishes are usually rather thick, but heating them makes them less syrupy and easier to apply (photo below). Wipe all excess oil from the surface. After the first coat is completely dry, smooth the surface with very fine sandpaper or steel wool and apply

a second coat. Once the wood has a uniform sheen, additional coats aren't necessary.

Most wipe-on finishes are blends of oil and varnish, so they're actually film-forming finishes. These blends also contain solvents to make them easy to apply and driers to make them dry quickly. Wear gloves, a respirator and maintain adequate ventilation.

Pure drying-oil finishes contain only tung oil or linseed oil. They have no added driers or solvents, so they're safer to use, but they dry very slowly.

Oil Finish

Cost: $14 to $25 per qt.

Coverage: 150 sq. ft.

Pros:
- Amber color adds warmth and depth
- Dust-, drip- and sag-free
- Easy to renew

Cons:
- Amber color highlights mottled figure
- Won't disguise color mismatches
- Dries slowly
- Oily rags are a fire hazard
- Sapwood remains light-colored
- Soaks into end grain and makes it dark

Heat oil finish in a bath of hot tap water to make it easier to apply. Keep the oil warm by occasionally changing the water.

Caution! Never heat finishes on your stove.

Film-forming finish keeps cherry from looking blotchy, but doesn't significantly enhance its tone. The cherry becomes richer looking on its own, as it ages under the finish. Within a year, it reaches a pretty coppery color.

Sprayed-on Film Finish

Finishes that harden into a film minimize cherry's mottled appearance because they have much less color than drying oils, and they don't soak in as much. The first coat of a film-forming finish seals the wood, so successive coats lay on top of each other. Each new coat thickens the finish film.

Spraying these finishes from an aerosol can is fast and convenient. It's great for getting into corners and covering intricate shapes. Spraying also eliminates brush stokes, and no brushes or rags makes cleanup simple. But, you do have to deal with overspray and nasty fumes. At $5 to $8 for an 11- to 12-oz. can, it's also kind of expensive.

You can find shellac, lacquer, and polyurethane in aerosol cans. I think shellac and lacquer look the best on cherry. Oil-based polyurethane dries the slowest, but it's the most durable. You can get a good-looking, durable finish by following an initial sealcoat of shellac with topcoats of polyurethane. Don't use waterborne poly. It leaves cherry looking pale and parched.

The secret with aerosol spray is to go easy (photo at right). Sanding off drips and sags from one heavy coat takes a lot more time than spraying and sanding two light coats.

Wear a respirator and maintain adequate ventilation any time you spray an aerosol finish. Here are some guidelines for aerosol spraying:

1. Keep the nozzle perpendicular to the surface and spray from a consistent distance, between 8 and 10 in. away.

2. Move the can at a steady rate. Start spraying before you reach the surface and don't stop until you're past it.

3. Move your project around (you may even want to turn it upside down) to get the best spraying angle. You can spray up and down as well as side to side.

It's easy to get in corners with aerosols because there's no brushing or wiping. Spray and sand between each coat.

Coping with Cherry's Light-Colored Sapwood

My best advice, which is to cut off all of the sapwood, isn't always practical. If you can't remove all of the sapwood, hide it on the underside or turn it to the inside whenever you can.

You can disguise sapwood with pigments or dye (photos below). These cover-ups look best when they're fresh. Here's why: Pigments retain their color over time, but dyes fade (water-based dyes last the longest) and cherry's color changes.

If you color sapwood with dye, it'll gradually get lighter while the surrounding heartwood gets darker. Matching the sapwood with pigment works better. Over extended lengths of time, however, exposure to sunlight can actually bleach cherry, so sapwood colored with pigment will end up being too dark.

The best way to color sapwood is to tone it with diluted golden-brown-colored dye, seal the surface with shellac, and glaze over with burnt-umber-colored pigment.

1 Sealed with shellac

Color sapwood with oil paint. First, seal the surface of the board with shellac. You may have to mix colors, to get a good match with the heartwood. Thinning isn't necessary. Brush the paint only on the sapwood.

2

Wipe the paint carefully, so you tone the sapwood without adding color to the heartwood. If you mess up, remove the paint with mineral spirits and try again.

Aerosol Film Finish

Cost: $5 to $8 per can

Coverage: 25 sq. ft.

Pros:
- Minimizes mottled figure
- Seals end grain so its color matches the face grain
- Fast drying (except oil-based poly)
- Easy to rub out (except oil-based poly)
- Polyurethane is most durable

Cons:
- Must sand between finish coats
- Possible drips, runs and sags
- Overspray
- Requires organic-vapor respirator
- Dust may stick to slow-drying polyurethane
- Won't disguise color mismatches
- Sapwood remains light-colored

4. Spray tough-to-reach areas first and areas that are most visible last.

5. Sand between coats with 280 grit or finer paper.

6. Use a new can for the final coat. Then you won't have to worry about a nozzle that spits because it's dirty or running out of finish.

Tip

An aerosol tip that sprays in a wide fan pattern is less likely to leave sags and runs. Just look at the nozzle. If it's round, it sprays a cone pattern; if it's rectangular, it sprays a fan. You can adjust fan-type nozzles to spray horizontally or vertically. Cans with fan-spray nozzles cost about a dollar more, but they're worth every penny.

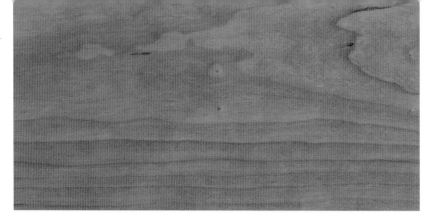

Shellac and glaze adds rich color and minimizes blotching. Shellac seals the wood so the glaze, which is thinned oil paint, adds color evenly. You can wipe the glaze hard, or feather it, leaving more in some spots than others. Glaze is great for disguising light sapwood.

Shellac and Glaze

The versatile shellac and glaze process is my favorite finish for cherry. It allows you to add color wherever it's needed, in a spot, or over the entire piece. It also helps to blend mismatched cherry boards or ply-wood and solid cherry. It disguises light-colored sapwood and hides mottling and unwanted curly figure. You can use it to make new cherry look older, because each coat of glaze deepens the color.

The technique is simple. First, apply a thin coat of shellac (Step 1). Sand it lightly, apply the colored glaze (thinned burnt umber artists' oil color—more on this later) and wipe it off. That's it. Because the shellac has sealed the wood, the color goes on evenly, without making the surface look muddy. Once you're satisfied with the color, topcoat with polyurethane.

If you have serious color mismatches to deal with, two-stage coloring may work best. Put a coat of golden-brown-colored dye on the unfinished cherry, before the shellac (see Sidebar, page 169). It tempers the color differences so they're easier to blend with glaze.

I like to brush shellac, but you can spray it, too. Sand each coat with 280-grit sandpaper (shellac takes about an hour to dry). Sand evenly and carefully, because glaze will accentuate any scratches and leave a dark line wherever you cut through the shellac.

Glaze is nothing more than thinned paint. I make glazes using artists' oil colors (Step 2). Artists' oils (see Sources, page 204) contain very finely ground pigments, so they don't look muddy, and you can match just about any wood by mixing colors. Liquid glazing medium (see Sources, page 204) makes the oil color spread evenly and dry faster.

Once you apply the glaze, you have plenty of time to work with it before it dries (Steps 3 and 4). It's also reversible (Step 5). Once the glaze is dry (overnight, in good conditions), you can deepen the color with a second coat, add additional glaze selectively to camouflage bad spots or highlight details, or finish with polyurethane. As with other finishes, cherry will continue to darken underneath the glaze, although you'll hardly notice it.

Seal the surface with dewaxed shellac. On cherry, a single thin coat (2 lb. cut) allows some glaze to lodge in the pores. This looks odd to me, because cherry's pores aren't naturally dark. Two thin coats, sanded between, keeps color out of the pores.

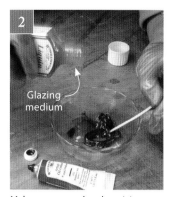

Glazing medium

Make your own glaze by mixing burnt umber artists' oil color and liquid glazing medium into a medium-bodied paste. You can get both at art supply or craft stores. Don't go overboard—a little glaze goes a long way.

Sealed surface

Cover the sealed surface with glaze. It doesn't matter how you apply it or if you miss a few spots. Wiping evens things out.

Use two rags for wiping, one that's fairly loaded with glaze and another that's fairly clean. Between the two you can feather the glaze however you want.

(Optional step) Mineral spirits removes glaze. If your glaze doesn't look right, you can take it off (before it dries) and try again.

Shellac and Glaze

Cost:

■ Shellac; $8 per qt

■ Glaze (artists' oil color and liquid medium); $15

■ Topcoat; $5 to $8 per aerosol can

Coverage: A little glaze goes a long way

Pros:

■ Rich color

■ Minimizes mottled figure

■ Goof-proof because it's reversible

■ Disguises sapwood

■ End grain matches face grain

Cons:

■ Additional steps take extra time

■ Added cost

■ Finish topcoats necessary

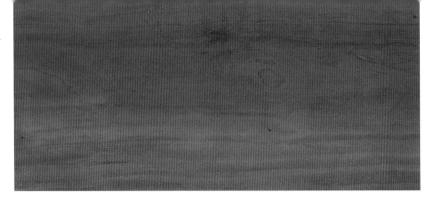

Age cherry instantly by chemical reaction. It takes decades for cherry to reach the deep red-brown color prized by antique lovers. But by treating new cherry with old growth's aging solutions today, you could fool most experts tomorrow. The process is simple and the results are eye-popping.

Chemical Reaction

If you're familiar with antique furniture, you know that aged cherry looks completely different from new cherry. It's very dark.

Finishers have been using chemicals to deepen cherry's color for eons, but the chemicals are dangerous to use and the results are unpredictable. Old Growth's aging solutions make the process safe (see Sources, page 204).

Their two-step application process is designed to produce consistent results.

The first solution leaves the surface of the wood evenly covered with a special mix of ionized minerals. When the second solution is applied, a chemical reaction occurs that permanently turns the cherry, including its light-colored sapwood, a much darker color.

You can decrease the intensity of the color change by diluting the activator solution with distilled water (Step 1). Don't dilute the catalyst solution—it has to go on full-strength (Step 2).

The surface doesn't need to be rinsed and the process doesn't raise the grain significantly. After the wood is dry, sand it lightly and apply clear topcoats of shellac, lacquer, or poly.

Darkening By Chemical Reaction

Cost:

- ▦ $22 for two 1-pt. bottles
- ▦ $1 for one gal. of distilled water

Coverage: 60 sq. ft.

Pros:

- ▦ Looks just like old cherry
- ▦ Easy and safe
- ▦ Makes sapwood the same color as heartwood

Cons:

- ▦ Highlights mottled figure
- ▦ Extra steps
- ▦ Finish topcoats necessary

1 Part activator

4 Parts water

Dilute the activator solution with four parts distilled water, and brush it on the cherry. When the activator is used full strength, the catalyst solution turns cherry a very dark color.

Activator solution applied previously

Sapwood

Brush on the catalyst solution, full strength, after the activator solution has dried. The cherry changes color immediately.

VERTICAL LUMBER ORGANIZER

by RICHARD HELANDER

Before I installed this vertical storage rack, my lumber was hard to manage and a housekeeping nightmare. I could never find the piece I wanted, and removing a board from the back of the stack was sure to cause trouble. Finally, after a major board slide, I decided to take action.

I drilled holes and installed 1-in.-dia. dowels in a 2x4 that I anchored to the wall. Mounting it diagonally allows me to separate my boards by length. Eye screws and chains help to secure them. A raised exterior-grade plywood shelf keeps the boards off the floor, so they don't absorb moisture from the concrete.

2x4 rail

1"-Dia. dowel

Before

EDITOR: TIM JOHNSON • ART DIRECTION: RICK DUPRE • PHOTOGRAPHY: RAMON MORENO, UNLESS OTHERWISE INDICATED

by DAVE MUNKITTRICK

4 Proven Finishes for Oak

MAKE THE MOST OF OAK'S CONTRASTING GRAIN

A good finish should highlight the best characteristics of the wood it goes on. I've put together four finish recipes that make the most of oak's contrasting grain. The first three recipes use two different color layers, each separated by a seal coat of shellac. Light penetrates and reflects back through the layers, giving these finishes stunning depth and beauty. The fourth is a simple, out-of-the-can recipe that produces a surprisingly good-looking finish.

The layered finishes start with a ground color of water-based dye. I like water-based dyes because they don't bleed back out of oak's pores like alcohol-based dyes do. Next, a barrier coat of dewaxed shellac seals in the dye. Shellac dries fast, allowing you to move through the steps quickly. A second layer of color, called a glaze, is applied over the sealed dye. The dark glaze fills the open-pored earlywood, increasing its contrast with the light-colored latewood. I use a gel stain for the glaze because it doesn't run all over or bleed back. Another coat of shellac seals in the glaze. The dewaxed shellac allows you to use your favorite topcoat. (Check out "Tips and Techniques for Fantastic Oak Finishes," page 176.)

ART DIRECTION: LISA PAHL KNECHT • PHOTOGRAPHY: PATRICK HUNTER

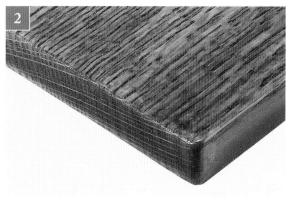

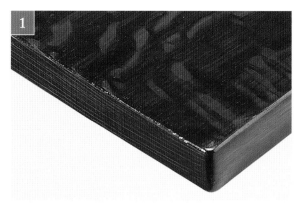

Mission Oak

This finish is designed specifically for quartersawn white oak. Sanding the dye coat ever so lightly really enhances the ray flecks.

1. Apply a 50-50 mix of Trans Tint Dark Mission brown and medium brown dye to the bare wood and let it dry.
2. Very lightly scuff-sand the dyed wood with 320-grit paper.
3. Seal the dye with a barrier coat of wax-free shellac.
4. Scuff-sand.
5. Glaze with Minwax walnut gel stain.
6. Seal with wax-free shellac and scuff-sand when dry.
7. Apply a topcoat of your choice.

Golden Oak

This is a classic oak finish familiar to any antique lover. The glaze layer darkens the open-pored earlywood and contrasts beautifully with the brownish-gold latewood. This finish looks best on red oak.

1. Apply J.E. Moser's Wizard Tints honey amber dye to the bare wood and let it dry.
2. Seal with shellac and scuff-sand when dry.
3. Glaze with Minwax walnut gel stain.
4. Seal with shellac and scuff-sand when dry.
5. Apply a topcoat of your choice.

Deep, Dark, Red Oak

This finish looks great on plainsawn red oak boards and is impossible to get straight out of a can. The red dye is incredibly strong. But the gel stain is applied without a barrier coat so it darkens both the earlywood and latewood.

1. Apply J.E. Moser's Wizard Tints bright scarlet to the bare wood and let it dry.
2. Apply Minwax jet black mahogany gel stain.
3. Seal with wax-free shellac and scuff-sand when dry.
4. Apply a topcoat of your choice.

Simple, But Nice, Oak Finish

This finish is as easy as it gets. Its results are not as spectacular as those of the other three recipes. But it makes up for its plainer look with ease of application.

1. Apply two coats of Rockler's Mission Oak Wipe-On gel stain.
2. Seal with shellac and scuff-sand when dry.
3. Apply a topcoat of your choice.

by DAVE MUNKITTRICK

Tips and Techniques for Fantastic Oak Finishes

THE BEST FINISHES CELEBRATE ITS FABULOUS GRAIN

Like a movie star, oak possesses natural good looks. Oak's distinctive grain pattern (see photo below) is what people are responding to when they say, "I love the look of oak." Unlike a movie star, however, oak is easy to work with—even during finishing. The best finishes for oak celebrate its grain. In this aricle, I'll highlight some key finishing tips and techniques used to create the multilayered finishes that bring out the best in oak. Check out the recipes that make use of these techniques in "4 Proven Finishes for Oak" on page 174.

Earlywood and latewood stain differently. Finishing oak is like finishing two different woods at once. The large, visible pores in the earlywood soak up stain much more aggressively than the relatively smooth latewood does.

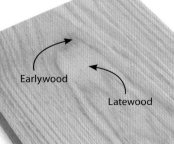

Earlywood

Latewood

ART DIRECTION: LISA PAHL KNECHT • PHOTOGRAPHY: PATRICK HUNTER

Avoid Disasters; Make Samples First

Always, always, always make samples before you begin to apply finish. Most finishing disasters can be avoided with this basic step. Making samples gives you the opportunity to tweak a recipe until you get the look you want. Be sure to make the samples out of scrap from the project you're finishing to get the most accurate preview of how the finish will look. Sand and finish the samples to the same level as your project and apply a topcoat.

Finally, accurately measure and record every step, including dye concentrations, mixture ratios, when to scuff-sand, number of topcoats, etc. There's nothing worse than hitting on the perfect look only to realize you don't know how you got there.

Key to a Good Finish: Proper Sanding

I sand oak to 220 grit. Although lots of people stop at 180 grit, I find going one more step really polishes the dense latewood and enhances its contrast with the coarse earlywood.

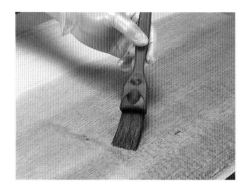

Create a Ground Color with Dye

Many great oak finishes begin with a "ground color" dye, typically a yellow or reddish brown. The ground color establishes the finish's predominate undertone. Apply the dye liberally to bare wood with a brush or spray bottle. Blot up any excess with a clean rag. Even when thinned to manufacturers' recommendations, dyes produce very strong colors. To avoid too strong a color or problems with lap marks, I recommend thinning the dye 50 percent beyond the bottle directions. You can always add a second or even third application of dye for a darker look, but it's a lot harder to go from dark to light.

Tip: I use a spray bottle to mist the wood with water before I put on the dye. The damp wood takes the stain more evenly than dry wood.

Add a Barrier Coat of Shellac

Shellac sealer brings the dyed oak to life. At the same time, it creates a barrier that prevents dyes or stains from bleeding into the next layer of finish. The barrier coat also creates distinct, well-defined layers that really add depth and beauty. Shellac is also used as a barrier coat between a colored glaze layer and the final topcoat. Be sure to use dewaxed shellac that's thinned to a 2-lb. cut. (A 2-lb. cut simply means 2 pounds of dry shellac flakes were dissolved in one gallon of alcohol.) This is a thin mix that's easy to brush and, because it's dewaxed, it's compatible with any topcoat. If you buy ready-mixed in the can, be careful: There are also cans of shellac labeled as a "finish and sealer" that use a more concentrated 3-lb. cut and contain wax. Read the label carefully. It should say something like "universal sanding sealer" and "100-percent wax-free formula."

Scuff-Sand Carefully

Scuff-sand with 280- or 320-grit paper between coats of shellac and varnish. A light touch is all that's needed. Care must be taken not to sand through one layer of finish into the next.

I typically scuff-sand after each coat of shellac. The sanding removes dust nibs and leaves a scratch pattern for the next coat to grip.

> **Tip:** Scuff-sand the dye coat on quartersawn oak to make the ray fleck really pop. Because the rays are so dense, the dye tends to sit on the surface where a light sanding can easily remove it. This makes the rays lighter than the surrounding wood.

Glaze Deepens the Grain Contrast

A glaze layer is the secret ingredient to a great oak finish. A dark glaze emphasizes oak's beautiful strong grain. Glaze is nothing more than a thick stain applied over a sealed surface. Apply the glaze with a stiff brush across the grain (see inset photo). This helps push the pigment deep into the wood's pores. The glaze is removed with a pair of rags. The glaze left in the open pores of the earlywood turns it very dark. At the same time, the sealed latewood takes

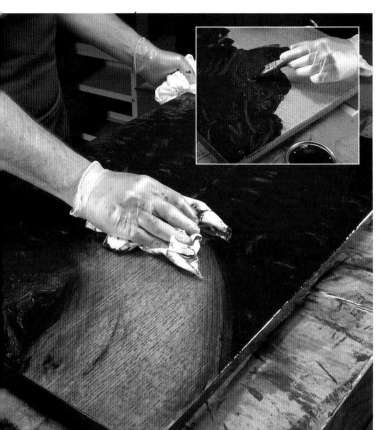

Topcoating Protects the Color

A protective topcoat adds depth and durability. Typical topcoats are oil-based or water-based varnish or lacquer. They protect the finish you've labored so diligently to create, as well as the wood beneath it. Be sure to seal the glaze layer before a topcoat is applied. Dewaxed shellac is the perfect sealer because it's compatible with any topcoat you choose.

up very little stain. The result accentuates the natural contrast in oak's grain. You can control the color strength on the latewood by either wiping the wood clean or leaving a little glaze behind. Use one rag to pick up the bulk of the stain. When it becomes saturated, it will leave a thin layer of color behind. Use the dry rag to clean up stain in corners or molding profiles. If the glaze ends up too dark or dries too quickly, don't panic; just wipe the surface with a rag soaked with mineral spirits and start over.

Tip: Cut the bristles of a disposable brush in half. The short, stiff bristles make it easy to scoop the thick gel out of the can and push the stain deep into the wood's open pores.

Projects for Special Wood

O nce you've got some very special wood, what are you going to make with it? Tables and wide panels are obvious choices. This section presents both plans and shop-worthy techniques to help you get from a pile of precious planks to a project that you can really be proud you made. You'll learn:

- how to make a table using a single precious plank as the top;
- how to flatten wide boards and slabs that won't fit through your 12-inch planer;
- how to lay out and cut book-matched panels from slabs of unusual wood, making the most of their color and figure;
- and finally, how to make a trophy coffee table using tree-wide slabs of wood.

❮ **Wow**—*Ever hear of English Burly Wych Elm? That's the beautiful slab this fellow has just made into a stunning table — and it's plain to see why he is so happy about it. That's what getting the most from your wood–buying bucks is all about: not pinching pennies, but making whatever money you have stretch into the stratosphere.*

by TOM CASPAR

Treasured Board Table

ONE PRECIOUS BOARD IS ALL YOU NEED

Every woodworker discovers an extraordinary piece of wood once in a while. What do you do with it? One board is not enough for a big project. It's a crime to cut it up into small pieces for a little project. So you stash it away, like a pirate burying his treasure, and wait for the perfect project. Here it is.

Turn your precious gem into an uncomplicated table for the hallway or behind the sofa. The thin black base recedes from view, leaving your beautiful wood to glow.

Our treasured board started out as a bigleaf maple growing on the western coast of Oregon. After it was felled by loggers, the tree laid on the forest floor and started to rot, or "spalt." Then it was hauled to a nearby river to be floated to the sawmill. It didn't make it to the mill. The log sank to the bottom of the river. Years later it was recovered from the river by a sawyer, cut into planks, and dried. Sunken treasure, indeed.

The base of the table is made from yellow poplar, a humble species of wood with green heartwood. While it may not be pretty, yellow poplar has appealing qualities. It's relatively inexpensive, even in thick planks. It's easy to machine and

sand, and its small pores fill quickly with finish, making a smooth surface to complement the top. Soft maple has the same characteristics and would be another good choice.

All the joints in this table are made with a plate joiner. The base is light in weight and won't be subject to much stress, so biscuits are a safe bet. The table rails are fairly thick. There's plenty of room for two #20 biscuits for each joint. All the rails and legs are made from the same piece of 6/4 lumber. (Make sure you have enough for a few extra legs.) The table's joints are staggered to keep the thin legs strong.

Preparing the Stock

Mill the wood for the base first, but don't take it down to final thickness and width right away. Leave it ⅛-in. oversize all round. Here's why: The legs are narrow pieces, and when they're released from a wide board they may bend or twist. Let them settle into a relaxed state over the course of a few days, then joint them again and mill to size. As for the rails, they should be allowed to relax too, because you're removing almost ½-in. of thickness.

Work on the top while you wait for the other wood to settle down.

The Top and Shelf

Your top may be made from one board or glued up from a couple of boards. In any case, take the time to compose it with care. If your board has been following you around for a while, that's great, because it has reached a state of equilibrium and

won't distort as you mill it. This table has no under structure to help hold a top flat, so you're relying on the stability of your special board.

Draw the slight curve of the top with a bent stick. Bandsaw the curve and chamfer the underside of the edge with a router (Photo 1). Stop before you make the final cut and fair the curves of the edge. This is easier to do now than when the edge was at its full thickness. Finish cutting the chamfer with a hand plane or belt sander.

Plane the shelf and cut it to width, but hold off on cutting it to length. You'll fit it to the base after the base is glued up. Then you'll draw the curves and smooth them off.

Chamfer the edge of the top with a router. Go around the top four or five times, lowering the bit for each pass. The chamfer will make the top seem thinner. Standard router bits cut a 45-degree chamfer. Increase the slope of the chamfer to 30 degrees to improve the floating effect, using a plane or belt sander.

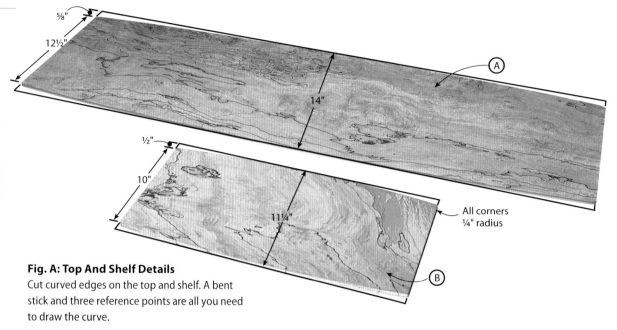

⅝"

12½"

14"

A

½"

10"

11¼"

All corners
¼" radius

B

Fig. A: Top And Shelf Details
Cut curved edges on the top and shelf. A bent
stick and three reference points are all you need
to draw the curve.

The Base

Mill all pieces to final thickness and width.
Taper the legs on two sides before cutting
the joints. With legs this small it's safer
to build your own tapering jig with toggle
clamps than to use a commercial jig that
forces you to hold the leg in place by hand
(Photo 2). Draw the taper on one leg in
order to set up the jig. Try it out on a spare
leg. You'll need a shim under one toggle
clamp when you cut the second taper.

Draw a centerline down the outside
face of each rail to locate the slots for the
biscuits. The four main rails are flush with
the inside of each leg. This means that the
inside face of the rail will be your reference
surface. Make sure the inside face is down
when you cut the slots.

Clamp the rail down to a truly flat
surface. Set your plate joiner on the work
surface to cut the first slot. Then place a

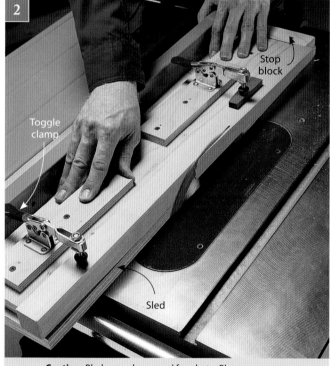

2

Stop
block

Toggle
clamp

Sled

Caution: Blade guard removed for photo. Please use yours.

Cut the tapered legs on the tablesaw. Hold the narrow leg in place with
toggle clamps mounted on a sled. This will keep your hands well away from
the saw blade. A stopper board at the foot of the leg prevents it from sliding.

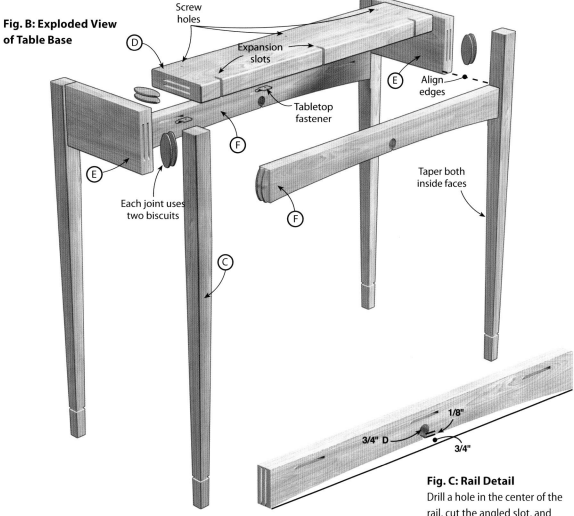

Fig. B: Exploded View of Table Base

Screw holes

Expansion slots

D

E

Align edges

Tabletop fastener

Each joint uses two biscuits

F

E

F

C

Taper both inside faces

1/8"

3/4" D

3/4"

Fig. C: Rail Detail

Drill a hole in the center of the rail, cut the angled slot, and bandsaw a slight curve to lighten the rail's appearance.

Cutting List
Treasured Board Table 46"L x 14"W x 27"H

Key	Qty	Part	Material	Th	W	L
A	1	Top	4/4 Maple	¾"	14"	46"
B	1	Shelf	4/4 Maple	½"	11¼"	23½"
C	4	Legs	6/4 Poplar	1¼"	1¼"	23½"
D	1	Upper Rail	6/4 Poplar	1³⁄₁₆"	5"	23½"
E	2	Side Rails	6/4 Poplar	1¹⁄₁₆"	4¼"	7½"
F	2	Front & Back Rails	6/4 Poplar	1¹⁄₁₆"	2⅝"	23½"

Hardware					
6	1¾" #10 pan head screws				
6	¼" washers				
6	tabletop fasteners				
6	½" #10 pan head screws				

⅜-in.-thick spacer under the machine and cut the second slot.

The front and back rails are as narrow as possible while still wide enough to hold a #20 biscuit. The slots go all the way from side to side and cut into the top edge of the rail a bit. That's fine, because these over-cuts will be covered by the shelf.

Mark the legs for slotting directly from the rails. Stand a side rail on a leg, flush with the top end, and transfer its centerline mark to the outside face of the leg. The front and back rails fit directly below the side rails, so it's easy to mark their positions (Photo 3).

Make a simple jig for slotting the legs. Hold the legs in place with the same toggle clamps you used for the taper jig (Photo 4).

Drill and shape the front and back rails. Round the lower edge with fine sandpaper. Mark the inside faces of all the rails. Sand the outside faces. Slot the front and back rails with your plate joiner for the tabletop fasteners (Photo 5).

Radius the edges of the side rails and legs on a router table using a ³⁄₁₆-in. round-over bit. Then smooth the surfaces. This will reduce the radius of the edges a bit. That's just what you want to happen on the legs, because the setback of the rails is also ³⁄₁₆-in., and you don't want the radius to come too close to the face of the rail.

Drill holes for screws to hold the top on one side of the upper rail. Slot the other side of the rail on the tablesaw. The slots allow the top to expand and contract without cracking.

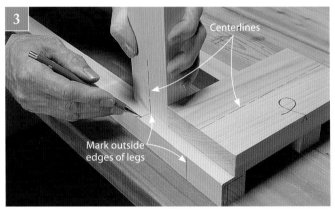

Lay out the biscuit slots with center marks. First mark the center of each rail. Then transfer the marks to the legs. Use the side rail as a spacer to determine where the front rail goes.

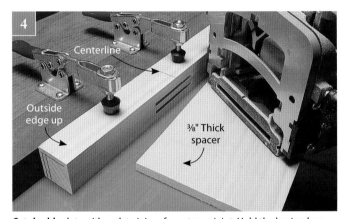

Cut double slots with a plate joiner for a strong joint. Hold the leg in place with toggle clamps mounted on a stiff board. Cut the first slot with the plate joiner flat on the work surface. Then raise the plate joiner with a ⅜-in. spacer to cut the second slot.

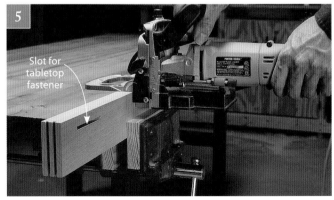

Cut slots for tabletop fasteners with the plate joiner. Reference with the fence set on top of the rail.

Glue-up and Finishing

Glue the ends of the table first. Biscuits don't align pieces side to side. You must do that yourself. Make sure the side rails are flush with the top ends of the legs before you apply clamping pressure. Have a mallet handy to knock the parts into place. You'll need pencil marks to align the top edges of the front and back rails. Square across from the bottom edge of the side rails to make these marks. Now you're ready to glue the rest of the table.

Prime the base by spraying on a sanding sealer. You will need one can. Sand with 220-grit paper. Color the base with a matte-black spray paint, such as Krylon 1613 Semi-Flat Black, (photo 6). You may need two cans of paint. Screw down the top, attach the shelf, and bring your buried treasure out into the light of day.

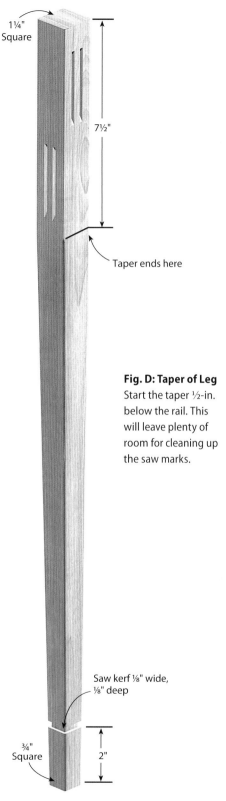

1¼" Square

7½"

Taper ends here

Fig. D: Taper of Leg
Start the taper ½-in. below the rail. This will leave plenty of room for cleaning up the saw marks.

Saw kerf ⅛" wide, ⅛" deep

¾" Square

2"

6

Fan

Respirator

Spray the base with matte-black paint. Wear a respirator and exhaust the paint fumes outside with a fan. Easy-to-sand red primer is used first to fill the pores and make a smooth surface. The thin, black lines of the base seem to disappear while the beautiful top springs to life!

by DAVE MUNKITTRICK

Flattening Wide Boards

YOU DON'T NEED MONSTER MACHINERY TO FLATTEN MONSTER BOARDS

Big, wide boards make my heart race with anticipation. Panels and tabletops are so pleasing to look at when they're made from a single board. Absent are jarring grain patterns and color changes caused by multiple board glue-ups. And I avoid the hassle of trying to match boards for a uniform, pleasing appearance.

I used to shy away from these beautiful wide boards because I thought I needed an aircraft carrier-sized jointer to flatten them. Over the years, I've learned a few tricks that allow me to take advantage of what a wide board has to offer—even in a small shop.

Don't limit your woodworking to boards that fit on your jointer or planer. Here are four tried-and-true techniques to tackle any size board with confidence.

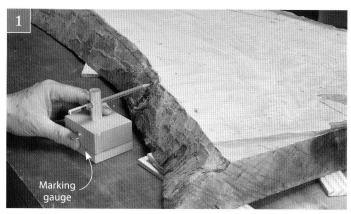

Flatten big slabs of wood in several steps. Place the board on a flat surface and add shims to steady the board. Use a shop-made marking gauge to transfer the flat surface onto the edge of the board.

Plane the high spots down to the line using a handheld power planer. First use a lumber crayon to mark the high areas. Skew the planer so the heel rides on the previously cut surface. Cut with the grain to avoid tear-out. Check your progress frequently with a straightedge.

Fine-tune the flatness of your board using winding sticks. When the two end sticks are parallel, run a third stick back and forth between the two to check for high areas in the middle. Mark any high spots and remove them with light cuts. Check your work frequently.

Power-Plane by Hand

For really wide boards, you'll have to abandon stationary machines. A handheld power planer is the key to this technique. First, you need a flat surface larger than the board. Shim the board under the high spots so it won't rock. A cupped board should be set convex side up at first to prevent rocking. Mark all four edges of a wide board with a marking gauge to indicate its high spots (Photo 1). The gauge is just a 2-in.-thick block with a ⅝-in. dowel set in a hole. Power-plane the board down to the marks (Photo 2). Use a set of winding sticks to fine-tune the flatness (Photo 3).

Big, thick planks are best flattened in stages. You don't want to remove all the wood at once. That's because removing wood releases tension, causing the board to slightly change its original shape. Remove about 75 percent of the wood you need to take off the first side. Then flip the board and remove another 75 percent. Let the wood sit for a day or two on stickers. Then re-mark and finish flattening the board.

If you're lucky enough to have access to a wide-belt sanding machine, you can get the finish-sanding done there. For the rest of us, a belt sander, a random-orbit sander (preferably a 6-in. model) and elbow grease will finish smoothing the board.

Joint & Hand-Plane

There's no need to cut an inch or two off a board's width so it'll fit your jointer. Instead, remove the jointer's guard and make a full-width pass (Photo 1). Then hand-plane the remainder (Photo 2). Now the board is ready for the planer. You may have to repeat the steps to get the whole length of the board flat.

Removing the jointer guard is no casual thing; you must take precautions! Clamp an acrylic guard to the fence to keep your hands clear of the cutterhead. And always, always use a pair of push blocks.

Caution: Secure a temporary acrylic guard over the cutterhead.

You can flatten a board that's slightly wider than your jointer by removing the guard. It's just like cutting a giant rabbet: The uncut portion rides over the rabbeting ledge on your jointer.

Hand-plane the uncut strip of wood flush. Skew the plane so its heel rides on the jointed surface of the board. A power hand planer will also do the job.

Rip a wide board into jointer-sized pieces on the bandsaw. Make sure the board has one straight edge to go against the fence. Make the cut where the grain runs straight on the board. That way, the joint will be less visible when the board is glued back together.

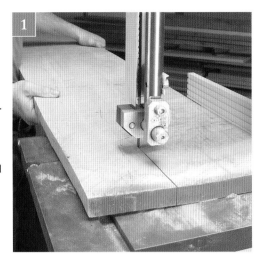

Rip, Joint & Reglue

If the board is more than 2 in. wider than your jointer, hand-planing is a chore. Try this technique instead: Joint an edge of the board and then rip it on the bandsaw (Photo 1). Joint and plane each board separately; then glue them back together (Photo 2).

To minimize grain interruption at the joint, it's important to avoid cutting through cathedral patterns. They're hard to align when the board is reassembled. Follow the straight grain and your joint will be almost invisible.

Glue the board together again after it has been jointed and planed. Leave the board a little thick so it can be planed to finish thickness after the glue dries. Shifting the boards a bit may help blend the grain and hide the joint.

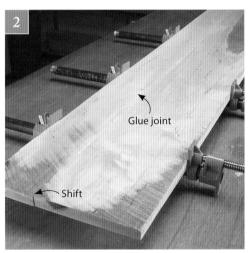

Glue joint

Shift

Turn Your Planer into a Jointer

Build a sled to hold a wide board steady through the planer (see photo, below). Fasten a stop at the front of the sled to keep the rollers from pulling the board through without the sled. Add a backerboard to prevent kickbacks. Shim under the high spots to prevent the planer rollers from flattening out the board before it's cut. You'll find it's best to position a cupped board concave side up because it's easier to shim around the perimeter than the middle of a board.

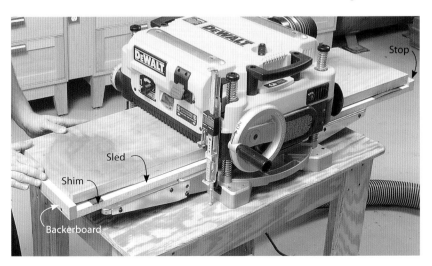

Stop

Sled

Shim

Backerboard

Joint a really wide board with your planer using a shop-made sled. Support the board on the sled with shims and double-faced tape. After you joint one side, remove the board from the sled and plane the second side normally. The sled is simply a piece of ¾-in. sheet stock. Stops and a backerboard are fastened to the ends to hold the board on the sled.

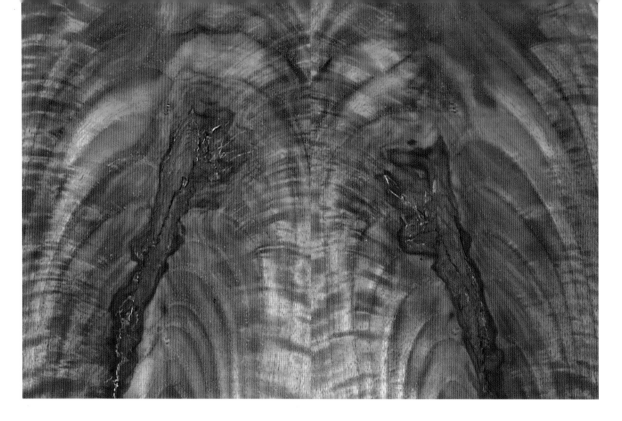

by SETH KELLER

Tips for Making Book-Matched Panels

SUCCEED WITH A TOUCH OF ARTISTRY AND SKILL

The longer I've worked with wood, the more I've appreciated that no two boards are alike. I like variety! But when I make a door panel or a cabinet side, I often want perfectly symmetrical boards: a book-matched pair in which the two boards mirror each other.

I make book-matched panels by sawing through the middle of a thick board, splitting it in two. It's just like opening a book—you never know exactly what you'll find inside! With the perfect board, the effect is stunning. Here are some tips to help you find those boards, to make the most of those that are seemingly too thin or too narrow and to glue them into striking patterns.

› Make Magic with a Mirror

My friends laugh about resawing magic, but I really do use a mirror before crosscutting and resawing a board into book-matched panels. By shifting the mirror, I can gain a fairly good idea how the finished panel might look. Angle the edge this way or that way? Crosscut here, or maybe down there? Just like a magic act, this mirror trick is really a lot of fun. I only wish the mirror could tell me what the inside of the board looks like. The outside is just a hint.

⌄ Align with Cauls

It's hard to clamp thin resawn boards together. The clamps won't stay on the edges. The joint pops apart. The seam won't stay even. Any of these situations can become a calamity if you've got glue on the boards, but cauls can save the day. Cauls are straight, stout boards that hold the panel rigid. Tape prevents the cauls from adhering to the panel. Here's the gluing order: First, put tape on the cauls. Next, apply glue to the two book-matched panels and butt them together. Clamp the cauls to the panel in opposing pairs. Finally, place clamps across the panels and squeeze the joint tight.

Caul

Masking tape

⌄ Think Inside the Board

Ignore the straight edges the sawmill gave you. If you can imagine new edges running at skewed angles to the factory ones, you can create spectacular mirror images.

This poor walnut board was cracked, had sapwood running down one side and featured an ugly bull's-eye figure. But it was crotch-wood, cut near a branch, with curly grain and dramatic colors. After I sawed new edges and split it open, look how splendidly it turned out (see photo, below). Wow!

EDITOR: TOM CASPAR • ART DIRECTION AND PHOTOGRAPHY: VERN JOHNSON

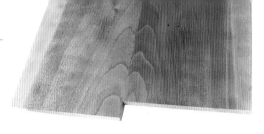

⌃ Make Panels Extra Long

Extra length makes it easier to align grain patterns by sliding one board past another. If you could cut a board with a knife, the way veneer is made, the grain on both boards would line up perfectly. But in the real world, sawing and jointing remove at least ⅛ in. between the boards. This lost wood means the boards' figure won't be identical.

Look at the edge of the board you'll resaw. The greater the angle at which the grain leans, the more offset the grain patterns will be. To be on the safe side, I usually roughcut the boards I'll resaw at least 2 in. longer than the panel's finished length.

After sliding one board past another, I look for good balance but don't expect all the figure to be perfectly aligned. I match the most prominent lines and disregard the rest.

› Add Thickness Before Sawing

Sometimes you have the perfect board for book-matching, but it's not thick enough. After bandsawing and planing, you might end up with a panel that's only ⅛ in. thick. This won't do, but don't toss that board away.

You can salvage the piece by gluing two more boards of the same species, one on either side, like a sandwich. Now you've got a thick board that's easy to resaw, joint and plane into two boards that are the thickness you need. The panel's back won't be book-matched, of course, but if it's a cabinet side, who's going to know?

› Mark the Ends

Do you ever get confused about what goes where? After machining a pile of resawn boards, I've had trouble identifying exactly which boards go together and which faces are the inside ones, the perfect matches. Sometimes an outside face can look suspiciously like an inside face.

To prevent this predicament, I now mark my boards with a cabinetmaker's triangle *before* I saw. This mark positively identifies the inner faces, because the triangle's halves can go back together only one way. I use different line patterns or colors to distinguish one board from another.

› Saw, Sticker and Stack

Patience pays off when making book-matched panels, whether they're large or small. After you saw, stack your boards in a pile. Separate each layer with stickers, so air circulates freely. Wait a few days before jointing and planing. This gives each board a chance to twist or cup if it wants to. These forces are virtually unstoppable, so it's better to give in than fight. Here's your consolation: This approach improves the chance that your book-matched panels will stay flat when installed in your project.

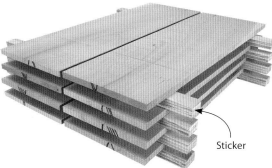

Sticker

˅ Seek Unusual Figure

Look twice at this panel—can you see an elephant's head? I didn't see this one at first, but boards with weird figure are often good candidates for resawing into book-matched panels.

Keep your eyes open for boards with swirly grain or knots near an edge or those whose figure runs out along an edge. When they're book-matched, the two mirror images make something new and entirely different, just like a folded ink blot. I prefer abstract patterns to elephants' heads, but children sure like this one.

Sand After Gluing

The high-tech way to level glued-up book-matched panels is to use a drum sander. If your boards have really wild grain from around a crotch or a knot, this is definitely the way to go. With a drum sander, there's no way you'll get tear-out.

› Add Width, Then Saw

What do you do if an ideal board isn't wide enough? Get out the board stretcher? I wish. No, the best solution is to edge-glue an additional piece before you resaw.

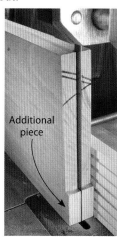

Additional piece

This works best when you're working with wood that has straight-grained figure. Straight grain glued next to straight grain can make a nearly invisible joint, particularly if the panels and the additional pieces come from the same parent board.

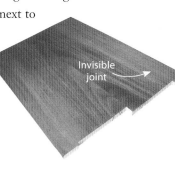

Invisible joint

by DAVE MUNKITTRICK

Trophy Coffee Table

STUNNING BEAUTY RIGHT FROM THE TREE

B ig planks of wood with natural bark edges make my heart race. Most woodworkers share a desire to build something from a single, thick plank of wood. After 20 years of building custom cabinets and furniture, I finally got my chance.

The first step was finding that perfect slab of wood—not an easy task. Slicing a tree into planks, bark edge and all, is not a common sawmill practice. I started my hunt in the Yellow Pages under "Sawmills." I found a number of people with portable mills, but without a log for them to saw, I was out of luck. I tried a few tree-trimming companies to see whether they had a tree trunk or two they needed to dispose of. Two strikes.

Finally, I turned to the Internet (Photo 1). I found the slab of my dreams: a huge (14- to 36-in.-wide x 12-ft.-long) slice of English Burly Wych Elm (pronounced "witch elm"). I knew immediately that this was the one. When the wood arrived at my door (Photo 2), I quickly realized that building with a single rough slab requires a completely different approach than working with individual boards.

On one hand, no decisions would be needed about grain pattern or color that individual boards require. With a single slab of wood, your only task is to present the natural beauty of the wood in the best way possible, despite all its inherent defects, such as loose bark pockets, rough edges, dirt, checks and cracks. On the other hand, just handling such an enormous yet delicate piece of wood presents some unique challenges.

1

I found the perfect plank for my coffee table on the Internet. It was a 12-ft.-long slab of Burly English Wych Elm. It was like no other piece of wood I'd ever seen. I couldn't wait.

2

The day the wood arrived, I had to call on a couple of neighbor friends just to get the crate in the shop!

3

Whoa! What a disappointment. The wood had the dull, grey appearance of a corpse. This wasn't what I was expecting.

I had a lot of fun building this table and you will, too, if you decide to build one like it. Because every natural-edged board is unique, it's difficult to give an exact formula on how to design or build a natural-edge table. Even if they come from the same tree, no two boards are alike. What follows is my experience as I built this table in front of the camera.

Arrival Day

After the wood was ordered, I couldn't wait for it to arrive. With all my thoughts on possessing that piece of wood, I neglected to plan ahead and be ready for its arrival. I discovered the hard way that you can't handle a large plank the way you can individual boards (Photo 2).

When we got the wood in the shop, I didn't let practical considerations slow me down. Totally intoxicated by what was inside the crate, I felt a burning desire to see the wood, now! We popped the bands and lifted off the protective cover. My heart sank at what I saw: an enormous slice of tree that looked more like clay than a beautiful figured piece of wood (Photo 3). A quick slosh of mineral spirits over the surface restored my spirits (Photo 4). The burl that grew around the Wych Elm tree came to life. Here was that amazing piece of wood I had seen on my computer screen. It was like no other piece of wood I'd seen before. It came from an old English estate and I can only imagine what the tree itself must have looked like—really, really gnarly. You could clearly see the normal grain of the elm in the center of the plank, but its edges were like one big, long burl. The swirling grain was punctuated by tight knots, each radiating small black cracks. The sight reduced us to a stunned stare. I knew we'd be able to breathe life back into this thing.

Broken Dreams

Of course, I had to see the other side of the plank as well. To avoid getting our fingers pinched as we turned the plank over, we let it drop. We heard a sickening crack and saw one of the beautiful burls lying limp at the plank's side (Photo 5). That's when this lesson finally hit home: you have to be very careful of the edges on a slab of wood like this. They are not only an integral part of the slab's character but are also very fragile.

Enough mistakes: I constructed a "plank train" (Photo 6) to safely handle my precious slice of tree. Now, the plank was mobile, the edges protected and the wood at a height where we could easily lift and turn it for inspection. To help season the plank to my shop air, I set 1¼-in. stickers under the plank and draped a polyester dropcloth over the whole thing (Photo 7). As we rolled the slab to the back of the shop, my mind was mulling over how to repair that broken piece of burl.

A slosh of mineral spirits gave us a glimpse of what to expect from the finished wood. My own spirits were restored; I really did have a treasure on my hands.

My hindsight kicked in. I built a "plank train" from shop carts and chipboard. Now, the plank was mobile, the edges protected and the wood at a height for easy handling.

Oops! In my excitement to see the other side, I managed to snap off a burl as we flipped the plank. I felt like a greenhorn.

It was time to let the plank acclimate to my shop for a few weeks. Stickers exposed both sides of the plank to the air. A plastic tarp slowed the moisture exchange.

Making the First Cut

After the wood sat for several weeks in the shop, I was ready to start work on the table in earnest. Now came the scary part: deciding where to cut the plank. Just the thought of making that irreversible step put beads of sweat on my forehead. Our wood had a wild edge all along its length. Still, there were natural breaks where it made sense to crosscut the slab.

This plank was about 36 in. at the butt end and only 14 in. at the top. I wanted to use the widest section for my coffee table. It promised the best proportions with a rich selection of burl on each edge. The rest of the plank would be used for a matching sofa table and the remainder sold to a friend to help defray the cost. It seemed like one cut could be made just past a check that ran up the center of the butt end and the second cut about 50 in. farther up the plank. I made preliminary marks to help me explore where these crucial cuts should be made (Photo 8). The plank dictated a wider coffee table than I had originally planned. Unlike making furniture from boards, you can't do much to adjust the size of your piece when it's a single plank. To be safe, I made a cardboard template of the proposed section and used it to check the fit in the room (Photo 9). Cardboard also made it easy to build and test different base designs. I settled on a simple design that's a snap to build with butt joints and screws (Fig. B, page 203).

Deciding where to make that first cut was nerve-wracking. I used chalk to rough out where the cuts might be made. I like chalk because it's easy to see and I can "erase" it with a stiff brush. The broken burl was set in place for reference.

I made a cardboard template of the proposed tabletop. I wanted to see how it would fit my living room. I also used cardboard to play around with base designs.

Edge Treatment

Now that I knew where I wanted to cut the plank, I wasn't sure how I wanted that cut to look. Should the cut be angled? Straight? Free-form? I tried a rough cut first (Photo 10). Then I textured the cut with a chisel (Photo 11). Hmm—it simply wasn't what I had in mind. I even used a jigsaw to cut a free-form edge and then a gouge to mimic the bark edge (Photo 12). I still wasn't happy. I finally settled on a straight cut polished smooth. I took advantage of a split at the butt end of the plank to create an offset cut (Photo 13). Two quick cuts with a circular saw freed my coffee table from the plank. I was glad to have a much smaller piece of wood to move around. At the same time, I felt a touch of sadness at breaking up that long plank.

Bark Side Up?

OK, next question: Which side of the slab should be up? There was a lot to consider here. Did I want the bark edge up, making it a prominent element, or down, tucked under the edge. I liked the overall look of the edge tapering back underneath the top edge. On the other hand, this plank had such gnarly bark, it was a shame to hide it. Neither side had a defect severe enough to tip the scales. After flip-flopping both the plank and my decision, in the end, I went with the bark side down.

Now that I knew where I was going to make the cuts, I had to decide how they would look. First, I tried rough and raw right from a chainsaw. It looked cool but too rustic.

I tried a little texture with a shallow gouge chisel, but it was a bit busy for my taste.

I even carved the end to mimic the free-form bark edge. It was fun to do, but it seemed a bit heavy-handed and fought for attention with the natural bark edge. I wanted some contrast.

Finally, I chose a straight cut sanded smooth to 220 grit. A little oil made it look like polished marble. I took advantage of a split at the butt end of the plank to create an offset cut.

I reattached the broken burl with epoxy. A board on top held the burl in place and wax paper kept the board from being glued to the plank. Padded clamps pulled the broken piece snug.

Fixing the Broken Burl

Now I turned my attention back to the broken piece of burl. Fortunately, the clean break would not require fancy repair work. Padded clamps applied enough pressure to hold the piece in place without damaging the burl edge (Photo 14). I needed a strong, gap-filling glue with a fair amount of open time to do this repair. I chose epoxy because it does not require a lot of clamp pressure and epoxy's gap-filling properties would fill the voids from any missing splinters of wood.

Making It Flat

I wasn't at all sure how I was going to flatten this monster board. Something crazy happened, though: I went to bed contemplating the problem and woke up with the answer. First I built a cradle in which to set the wood (Fig. A, page 203). The slab was shimmed up under the high spots so it wouldn't rock (Photo 15) and wedged in place so it wouldn't move (Photo 16). Then I fashioned a router carriage out of aluminum channel. The carriage rode on top of the rails and guided the router as it passed back and forth over the plank (Photo 17). I used a special bit called a bottom-cleaning bit (see Sources, page 204). The bottom-cleaning bit cuts on both the bottom and the side. The bit's 1¼-in. diameter helped shorten the duration of an odious task.

The next task was flattening the rough plank. I built a simple cradle to hold the rough wood. Shims supported the slab and kept it from rocking.

I wedged the wood in the cradle to keep it from moving around.

Starting with the bit set about ⅛-in. below the highest point on the plank, I began to flatten the board. I stepped the bit down in ⅛-in. increments until the whole surface was flat. Then I flipped the plank and milled the reverse side.

Fixing Defects

Most of the cracks were small and added to the wood's natural beauty. Nevertheless, I wanted to fill a few stress cracks that ran across the plank's grain. I used epoxy to fill the largest cracks (Photo 18). It dries to an amber color and blends well with a natural finish. I added a cellulose filler to give the epoxy more body so it wouldn't run out of the cracks.

Cleaning Up the Bark Edge

I found a nylon brush attachment for my drill to be the perfect tool for cleaning the bark edge (Photo 19). The stiff nylon brushes are embedded with an abrasive. They work to remove loose bark and dirt without scoring the wood like steel brushes do.

Sanding It Smooth

To smooth the top surface, I turned to my 4-in. belt sander (Photo 20) followed by my random-orbit sander. I started with an 80-grit belt and diagonal strokes for the initial sanding. I followed that with a 120-grit belt running with the grain. Then I switched to a 6-in. random-orbit sander. I backed up one grit when I switched from the belt sander to my random-orbit sander. Then I worked through the grits all the way to 220 grit.

I used a router in a sliding carriage to flatten the top. A wide bit made the task a little less tedious.

Before sanding the top, I reached for the epoxy again, this time to fill a few unsightly cracks. Epoxy blends well with the natural finish I was planning to use.

An abrasive-impregnated nylon-bristle brush worked beautifully to clear away loose bark and dirt from the edges.

A belt sander followed by a random-orbit sander smoothed the top.

I decided to make a simple plywood base that wouldn't compete visually with the top. I fastened it to the top through cleats screwed onto the base's top edge.

Fig. A: Flattening Carriage
Use jointed 2x4s that have dried in your shop to start the base. Add a piece of sheet stock about 2 in. wider than the widest section of your plank. The rails need to be dimensioned so they are slightly taller than the thickness of your slab. Space the aluminum channel about ⅛ in. wider than the base of your router.

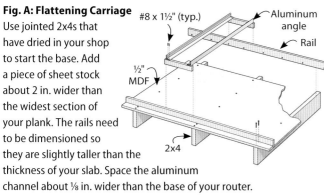

#8 x 1½" (typ.)
Aluminum angle
Rail
½" MDF
2x4

Fig. B: Base
The base is sturdy, easy to build and unobtrusive. It's made from doubled-up plywood. Support wings are screwed to a main spine that runs diagonally along the length of the slab. This base design can be adapted to any shaped slab of wood.

Cleat
#8 x 2" (typ.)
4"
16"– 18"
Plug
Doubled up ½" ply

Finishing the Top

I wanted a clear finish that could be applied to the gnarly bark edge without pooling and dripping. I chose a wipe-on polyurethane because it's applied like an oil finish but it dries hard. It was easy to work into the bark edges. Daubing the wet bark with a dry rag was all it took to clean up the excess finish. Be sure to put as many coats on the bottom as you do on the top.

Attaching the Base

I screwed the base to the top through cleats glued along the base's top edge (Photo 21). At the outside edges where grain movement is an issue, I drilled oversized holes and used washer-head screws.

Sources

Dyes and Stains

Homestead Finishing Company
TransTint Dyes
(216) 631-5309
www.homesteadfinishingproducts.com

Epoxy

Epoxy Heads
(866) 376-9948
www.epoxyheads.com

System Three
(253) 333-8118
http://www.systemthree.com

Fasteners

Horton Brasses
(800) 754-9127
www.hortonbrasses.com

Moisture Meters

Electrophysics
(800) 244-9908

Protimeter
(800) 321-4878

Wagner
(800) 944-7078

Pore Fillers

Compliant Coatings
California (800) 696-0615

Constantine's
(800) 223-8087
www.constantines.com

Reclaimed Timbers

American Timbers Co.
Maryland (800) 461-8660

Banducci and Evenson
California (707) 629-3679

Traditional Woodworks
Wisconsin (800) 882-2718

Trestlewood
Utah (877) 375-2779

Vintage Log and Lumber
West Virginia (888) 480-4372

Shellac

WoodFinishingSupplies.com
(866) 548-1677
www.woodfinishingsupplies.com

Wood Stabilizer

General Finishes
Sealacell Step 1
(800) 888-8286
www.generalfinishes.com

P.C. Petrifier
(800) 220 2103
www.pcepoxy.com

Wood Suppliers
Cedar Canyon Woodworks
(512) 331-7978
www.flash.net/~ccwdwrks

Certainly Wood
(716) 655-0206
www.certainlywood.com

Hearne Hardwoods
(888) 814-0007
www.hearnehardwoods.com

Northwest Timber
Oregon (541) 327-1000
www.nwtimber.com

Quality Hardwoods
(517) 566-8061
www.qualityhardwoodsinc.com

Randel Woods
Washington (360) 497-2071

Talarico Hardwoods
Pennsylvania (610) 775-0400
www.talaricohardwoods.com

Texas Kiln Products
(512) 360-4385
www.texaskilnproducts.com

WCW Mesquite
(830) 426-3000

West Penn Hardwoods
(888) 636-9663
www.westpennhardwoods.com

Yankee Veneer Corp.
(877) 355-8957
www.birdseyemaple.com

Discover these other great books from American Woodworker and Fox Chapel Publishing

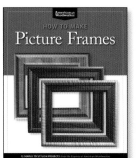

How to Make Picture Frames
11 Simple to Stylish Projects from the Experts at American Woodworker
Edited by Randy Johnson

Add a special touch to cherished photos and artwork with these easy-to-make picture frames.

ISBN: 978-1-56523 – 459-8
$19.95 • 120 Pages

How to Make Bookshelves and Bookcases
20 Outstanding Storage Projects from the Experts at American Woodworker
Edited by Randy Johnson

Build functional yet stylish pieces from a simple wall shelf to a grand bookcase. Features step-by-step instructions, cut-lists, and complete diagrams.

ISBN: 978-1-56523-458-1
$19.95 • 160 Pages

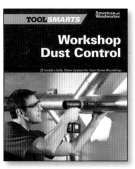

Tool Smarts: Workshop Dust Control
Install a Safe, Clean System for Your Home Woodshop
Edited by Randy Johnson

Get wood dust under control with expert advice on shop vacuums, dust collectors, and air scrubbers. Includes handy tips for making tools work cleaner.

ISBN: 978-1-56523-461-1
$19.95 • 128 Pages

Illustrated Cabinetmaking
How to Design & Construct Furniture that Works
By William H. Hylton

The most complete visual guide to furniture construction ever published! Includes hundreds of drawings, and exploded diagrams.

ISBN: 978-0-76210-183-2
$24.95 • 374 Pages

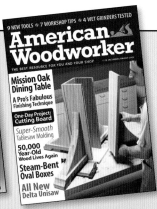

American Woodworker

With American Woodworker, you'll know what the experts know. No other woodworking magazine gives you so many exciting projects, expert tips and techniques, shop-tested tool reviews and smart ways to improve your workshop and make your shop time more satisfying.

Subscribe Today!
Call 1-800-666-3111 or
visit Americanwoodworker.com

Look For These Books at Your Local Bookstore or Woodworking Retailer
To order direct, call **800-457-9112** or visit *www.FoxChapelPublishing.com*

By mail, please send check or money order + $4.00 per book for S&H to:
Fox Chapel Publishing, 1970 Broad Street, East Petersburg, PA 17520